Countless thanks go out to the people who were involved in the development of this SAT®
Study Guide:

Arielle Woronoff

Personalized Test Prep
featuring the Test Genome Project

About the Authors

Patrick Bock, the founder of Specifix Prep, has over 16 years of experience helping students master the SAT and ACT. While spending 10 years as a teacher, tutor and content developer for one of the big guys, Patrick recognized the weaknesses of the "one size fits all" approach offered by larger test prep companies and the limitations of the strictly academic approach of smaller companies.

He also believes that a great SAT program must have the ability to determine a student's specific issues quickly and accurately. Patrick has a deep understanding of the SAT. He is obsessed with honing his teaching skills, constantly refining and adjusting his methods so each lesson is better than the last.

Jay Casale has been working with SAT and ACT students for the better part of 8 years. Over this long and winding road of test preparation, he has learned that acing the tests requires more than just the mastery of tricks and strategies. Jay feels that test prep should go a long way toward creating a well-rounded student.

Jay's passion lies not only with helping students to gain acceptance to college, but also to appreciate the process of learning, so that they can achieve success once there. He firmly believes that the unique tools and materials available to Specifix Prep's students are second to none because they provide both instructors and students with detailed, accessible, and wholly useful content and strategies.

Introduction

Math

Reading

Writing & Language

Review

Five Things to Know About the SAT

Before we get started, there's something we need to get out in the open:

Cramming a ton of effort into a few months of preparation is not going to make up for years of goofing off in school. If you don't pay attention in school and are hoping to rock the SAT, this book is probably not for you. No magic tricks, no silver bullets.

However, if you do well in school and just don't see the same level of success on standardized tests, this book is for you. We love working with students like you.

OK, sermon is over. Now we can start...

ostensibly: adv., apparently or purportedly, but perhaps not actually

1. This is not a school test.

The SAT is *ostensibly* a reasoning test. However, this characterization is incomplete. A more accurate description is this: **the SAT measures how well you take the SAT**. It does this by playing by its own rules. Learn the rules, and improve your score. Simple.

As mean as your teachers may be, they still want you to do well. The College Board and ETS, on the other hand are not your friends.

The test writers are not educators. They're not teachers. And they're certainly not committed to your educational success. They're a lot more interested in taking advantage of the way a typical student responds to specific stimuli. Predictability will get you in trouble quite frequently on this test. Learning more about the test works will keep you from making careless mistakes or taking unnecessary risks.

2. Your score is the result of a combination of your concept mastery, technique mastery, and conscientiousness.

Concept Mastery refers to the stuff you just need to know to answer a question correctly (e.g., there are 180 degrees in a triangle; *ostensibly:* (adv.) outwardly appearing in a certain way; the present perfect verb tense refers to an action completed prior to the present). There are over 400 different concepts present on any particular administration of the SAT. Chances are you don't know them all. This book is designed to teach you the things you don't know.

Technique Mastery means knowing the best way to handle each question type. A high level of technique mastery allows you to move through the test more efficiently and approach each

1

question in a calm, systematic way. This book will teach you every technique you'll need for every question type on the test.

Conscientiousness refers to your ability to be thorough, careful, and vigilant. It implies a desire to do a task to the best of your ability. The SAT is going to challenge you in ways you have never been challenged before. The degree to which you can calmly think through your difficulties and diligently apply what you will learn is going to make a huge difference.

You can probably tell by now you have a lot of work ahead of you. Improving your score on the SAT will be hard work. That's ok. Getting good at pretty much anything is hard work. Getting a great SAT score will open a lot of doors for you and is certainly worth the effort you put in.

3. Guessing is Good.

You probably already know this, but the SAT has no guessing penalty. Don't leave any questions unanswered. We're going to be using a Two-Pass system here.

First Pass

Answer the questions you know how to do. Skip over the ones that you think you might be able to handle, but will take a while or require accessing information in the deep recesses of your brain to answer. Circle these items so you don't have to look for them on your second pass.

Second Pass

Tackle the items that you circled on your first pass. Anything, go ahead and guess after eliminating any answer choices you think are wrong. Guess the same letter all the way down or guess randomly. It doesn't matter.

4. Speed is your enemy.

The way the test is scored is really important to your strategy. You can get a really good score and not answer every question. Indeed, answering every question is a really bad idea unless you're shooting for over a 700 in each section. You can learn exactly how many questions you are allowed to guess on from the chart below (these numbers are for the ENTIRE TEST).

If you're shooting for a...	Guess up to this Many Questions		
	Reading	Math	Writing
750-800	6	4	4
700-750	10	8	5
650-700	13	14	7
600-650	17	19	12
550-600	29	26	17
500-550	32	32	20
450-500	38	38	25
400-450	43	42	29

First, create a goal score for each section. To keep your goals realistic, add 50-100 points to each of your previous SAT or PSAT scores (add a zero to the end of each of your PSAT scores).

Section	Current Score	Goal Score
Reading	_____	_____
Math	_____	_____

Find your goal score and memorize the appropriate numbers. You may see that you can guess on quite a few questions. This will allow you to slow down and increase your accuracy on the questions that you do answer. Remember this: **Slow is smooth and smooth is fast.** These are important principles. You'll receive occasional reminders of these as the lessons progress.

5. To improve your score, you will have to change.

If you don't significantly alter the way you approach the test, don't expect your score to budge. This book will encourage you to think about how you think (learning experts call this metacognition) and understand why you're not getting the score you deserve.

Insanity: doing the same thing over and over again and expecting different results.
-Albert Einstein

Goal Setting and Time Management

What is a good score?

Well, it's the best score you can get given a reasonable amount of effort and prep time. Since you have this book in your hands, it's clear you're interested in improving your scores. How much you can hope to improve is going to be a function of several factors:

1. **Your Starting Scores**

   A dramatic score improvement is more likely if you're starting from a 400 than if you're starting from a 650. Plan accordingly.

2. **Time Spent Studying**

   If you think that you can improve your score by answering a random question here or there, you're fooling yourself. How much time that you spend each night studying is important, but so is how time on the calendar you devote. Months are better than weeks.

3. **The Nature of Your Issues**

   Do you have a solid foundation of content mastery but just stink at taking tests? Are you a good test taker but don't know the rules? Are you careless or careful? Some issues take longer to fix than others.

4. **How Stubborn You Are**

   Getting better at taking the SAT means changing the way you think and getting over bad habits. Have some humility and admit you don't know everything – you'll be amazed how much it helps.

5. **Whether You Suffer from Test Anxiety**

   Test anxiety is a physiological response to psychological stress. It sucks. Practicing under real test conditions is the name of the game here.

Whatever your issues, it's a good idea to set a goal score – something you'd be happy with *that's also realistic*. Your current scores are a good place to start.

Current Scores	**Goal Scores**
Verbal: _____	Verbal: _____
Math: _____	Math: _____

Now let's use your goals to create a time management strategy. First off, how many questions are you going to need to answer correctly?

SAT Pacing Goals

To score...	Critical Reading # Correct	Writing and Language # Correct		To score...	Math # Correct
400	16	16		410	16
420	17	17		420	17
420	18	18		430	18
440	19	19		440	19
450	20	20		450	20
460	21	21		460	21
470	22	22		470	22
480	23	23		490	25
490	24	24		500	26
500	25	25		510	27
510	26	26		520	28
530	27	27		530	30
540	28	28		540	31
550	29	29		550	32
570	30	30		560	34
580	31	31		570	35
590	32	32		580	36
600	33	33		590	37
610	34	34		600	38
620	35	35		610	40
640	36	36		620	41
650	37	37		630	42
660	38	38		640	43
670	39	39		650	44
690	40	40		660	45
700	41	41		670	47
720	42	42		680	48
740	43	43		690	49
750	44	44		700	50
760	45	44		710	51
770	46	44		730	52
770	47	44		740	53
780	48	44		750	54
780	49	44		760	55
790	50	44		780	56
800	51	44		790	57
800	52	44		800	58

Now that you know how many questions you need to answer correctly to reach your goal scores, what should you do with that information?

The Two-Pass System

Have you ever spent a ton of time on a question (like, way too much time), only to get that question wrong? Did, at some point, you think to yourself, "I have already spend two minutes on this question – I kind of have to finish it now."?

If so, you have fallen victim to the **Sunk Cost Fallacy**.

> "The...term *sunk cost fallacy* has been used by economists and behavioral scientists to describe the phenomenon where people justify increased investment of money, time, lives, etc. in a decision, based on the cumulative prior investment ("sunk costs"), despite new evidence suggesting that the cost, beginning immediately, of continuing the decision outweighs the expected benefit."
>
> *Source: Escalation of commitment - https://en.wikipedia.org*

Congratulations. You have joined the ranks of car owners who dump money into fixing an old jalopy instead of investing in a new car, the investors behind nearly every app on your phone, the agencies behind the war on drugs, and the politicians responsible for the Vietnam War. Damn. That escalated quickly.

Anyway, the point of all this is DON'T BECOME FIXATED ON ANY SINGLE QUESTION UNLESS YOU HAVE SEEN EVERY ITEM IN THE SECTION. One of the big tragedies of the SAT is that so many students run out of time before they get to questions they'd be able to answer correctly.

To make this easier, you'll be using the Two-Pass System

First Pass

Every question is worth one raw point. On your first pass, answer every question you're at least reasonably confident about. That means any question that you think you can answer in less than two minutes. Skip any questions that you either don't understand, contain concepts or vocabulary that you're a little foggy on, or questions you think you can do but will require a bit more time.

If you're able to hit your target on this pass, great. If you're close, don't worry. There are more points to be had. If you're nowhere near your target, you may want to consider revising your goals.

Second Pass

You're mopping up here. Since you will have already seen every question, use this pass to spend a bit more time on questions that you knew were going to give you trouble and guess on the questions that you don't understand.

Remember, there is no guessing penalty, so make sure you have every oval filled in. Except on the grid in questions. That would be crazy.

And don't do this:

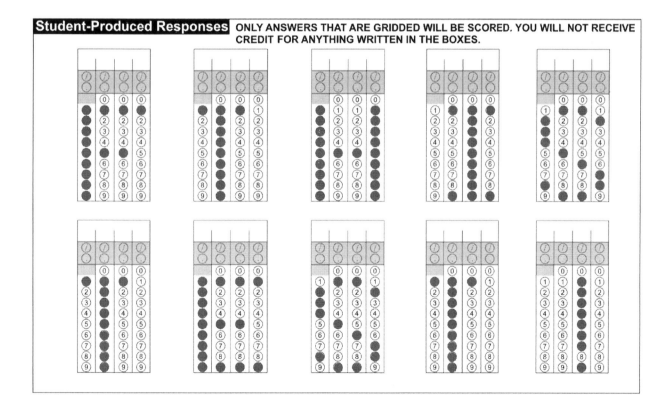

Working Smarter with the Answer Choices

QUESTION: What do the following two questions have in common?

What is the largest European country that borders only one other country?

Who holds the World's Record for longest name?

Stuck? Compare them to these:

What is the largest European country that borders only one other country?

- A) Portugal
- B) Switzerland
- C) Canada
- D) Qatar

Who holds the World's Record for longest name?

- A) Adolph Blaine Charles David Earl Frederick Gerald Hubert Irvin John Kenneth Lloyd Martin Nero Oliver Paul Quincy Randolph Sherman Thomas Uncas Victor William Xerxes Yancy Zeus Wolfeschlegelsteinhausenberdorft, Senior
- B) Captain Fantastic Faster Than Superman Spiderman Batman Wolverine The Hulk And The Flash Combined
- C) Barnaby Marmaduke Aloysius Benjy Cobweb Dartagnan Egbert Felix Gaspar Humbert Ignatius Jayden Kasper Leroy Maximilian Neddy Obiajulu Pepin Quilliam Rosencrantz Sexton Teddy Upwood Vivatma Wayland Xylon Yardley Zachary Usansky
- D) X O

These are all real names. The world is a crazy place.

ANSWER: They're easier to answer when you have Answer Choices!

Some questions on the SAT are difficult because we're not used to working with multiple-choice tests, particularly in Math and Reading. But those same questions can be made much easier by remembering that one of the five answers that are provided *has* to be correct. We'll explore this idea in more detail later, but keep it in mind.

> When was the last time you took a
> multiple-choice test in English class?

How would having answer choices make the following question easier to answer?

14

Bobby lost half his marbles, then gave away three,
then doubled his marbles, and ended up with 10
fewer marbles than twice what he had started with.
How many marbles did he start with?

QUESTION: What do the following questions have in common?

What is your favorite thing to do when you get home from school?

A) get started on homework
B) clean your room
C) read a book
D) rake/mow the lawn

What is a synonym for the word *direct*?

A) mercurial
B) unequivocal
C) pragmatic
D) ambivalent

ANSWER: They're easier to answer in YOUR OWN WORDS! That is, having Answer Choices makes the questions *more* difficult.

Some questions on the SAT are harder because you're NOT using the Answer Choices. Other questions are harder because you ARE using the Answer Choices. Being a good test taker means knowing how to use this knowledge to your advantage.

Good to Use Answer Choices	Bad to Use Answer Choices
Math	Reading
Writing & Language Arts	

You'll learn more about this as you work your way through this book.

Know the Rules

There is no substitute for just plain knowing the rules. You can have the best strategy in the world, but that's not going to help you if the question feels like it's written in a different language. Part of doing well on the SAT is having rock-solid *Content Mastery*.

Let's consider a few examples.

Math

Almost 40% of the questions on the Math section can only be answered by applying very specific concepts. For these questions, no flashy technique or strategy on Earth will guarantee the correct answer. You have to **Know the Rules**.

For example…

How many degrees are in a hexagon?

What's the difference between a ratio and a fraction?

How do you find the length of a leg of a square given its diagonal?

What's the relationship between the radius of a circle and a tangent line?

These are simple examples. Let's look at a question and consider two possible approaches: one in which the test taker *doesn't* know the rules and one in which he *does*.

"Don't wish it were easier. Wish you were better."
- Jim Rohn

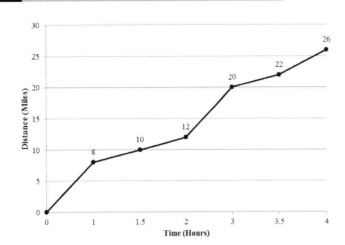

The figure above shows the position, measured at random intervals, of a runner over the course of a race. According to the figure, what is the runner's average speed, in miles per hour, for the entire race?

A) 5
B) 5.5
C) 6
D) 6.5

A Student Who Doesn't Know the Rules

"Yeesh. To find average speed, I think I'll have to find all the speeds and then take the average of them. So for the first hour, he ran 8 miles in an hour, and $speed = \frac{distance}{time}$, so 8 mph. For next part, he ran 2 more miles (did he get a cramp?), so 4 mph. This is easy. Next, 4 mph. From hours 2 to 3, 8 mph again. Next, 4 mph again. Finally, 8 mph. The average of 8, 4, 4, 8, 4, and 8 is 6. Boom. Circling C)."

A Student Who Know the Rules

"Well, I know that $average\ speed = \frac{total\ distance}{total\ time}$. This is easy. $\frac{26}{4} = 6.5$. I'm choosing D). I would like my points, please."

See the difference?

Reading

Knowing the rules on the Reading section is mostly about knowing what words mean. Vocabulary is super important here. Less common – but just as important – will be your ability to ascertain an author's tone or style based on the connotations of the words he or she chooses. More on that later. Let's look at an example.

5

…The nonpartisan legislative committee found the politician's actions reprehensible and thus unanimously voted to publicly censure him….

The writer's tone while describing the committee's reaction to the politician's actions can best be described as:

A) provident
B) dispassionate
C) outraged
D) sympathetic

A Student Who Doesn't Know the Rules

"Yikes. I don't know what a lot of these words mean. I think *censuring* means to cover up something objectionable or offensive, so C) makes the most sense. But I know that the test likes to trick me with words that sort of look like words I know, so it might be the opposite, so D) might be right. Wait, is there any tone? Ugh. I think I'll guess…"

A Student Who Know the Rules

"Well, I know a *nonpartisan* committee is supposed to be objective, and that *censuring* means to publicly rebuke someone, but those words apply to the committee, not the writer. Seems like the tone is neutral, so I'm going to go with B). Piece of cake."

Writing and Language

Most of your Writing score is going to depend on your grammar knowledge. Again, if you know the rules, you're in business. If you don't, you're going to have a tough time. Take a look.

There is probably no story more dramatic than San Francisco's first openly gay mayor and human rights activist, Harvey Milk.

5

A) NO CHANGE
B) then
C) than that of
D) then that of

A Student Who Doesn't Know the Rules

"I don't see anything wrong with this. I'm picking A)."

A Student Who Know the Rules

"This is a Faulty Comparison. I'm picking C)."

There's no way to solve questions like these without knowing the appropriate rules. The Comprehensive Skills Assessment identified the rules you don't know. Learn them by working your ways through the modules.

SAT Math

#	Section 3	Section 4
1		
2		
3		
4		
5		
6	Multiple Choice	
7		
8		
9		
10		
11		
12		
13		Multiple Choice
14		
15		
16	Student Produced Responses	
17		
18		
19		
20		
21		
22		
23		
24		
25		
26		
27		
28		
29		
30		
31		Student Produced Responses
32		
33		
34		
35		
36		
37		
38		

There are 58 math questions on the SAT.

The questions follow a predictable order of difficulty: the higher the number, the more difficult the question. Easy questions have straightforward solutions, and difficult questions have less obvious solutions. Remember this so you don't over- or under-think a question.

SAT Math Topics

Questions on the Math section will fall into the following categories:

- **Algebra**
  - algebraic manipulation, order of operations, simultaneous equations, translating English to algebra, inequalities, quadratic equations, factoring polynomials, the quadratic equation, completing the square
- **Arithmetic**
  - ratios, proportions, rate, probability, combinations and permutations, patterns, sequences, percentages, fractions, exponential growth/decay
- **Geometry**
  - plane geometry, coordinate geometry, solid geometry
- **Functions and Graphs**
  - finding parts of a function, transformations, reading an xy-coordinate plane, slope, linear functions, parabolas, conics and ellipses
- **Trigonometry**
  - SOHCAHTOA, basic identities
- **Data and Statistics**
  - mean, median, mode, standard deviation, interpreting bar graphs, line graphs, pie charts, tables, pictographs, and scatter point plots
- **Number Properties**
  - rules of exponents, properties of fractions, positive/negative numbers, integers, number lines, absolute value, rules of one and zero, odds and evens
- **Visual Perception**
  - visual manipulation

This is good news. Most of these should be concepts you have learned already. The SAT a test of math you know.

There's even more good news:

You will NOT see the following types of questions:

- **Advanced Functions**
- **Geometric Proofs**
- **Advanced Trigonometry**
- **Calculus**

When people say that they're bad at math, they're usually referring to this second group of concepts. Almost everyone struggles with them. You should find the fact that they're not on the SAT quite encouraging.

But the point of this discussion isn't to highlight how easy or awesome the SAT is, but rather to explain how ETS is able to take ostensibly straightforward concepts and turn them into something much more sinister.

Want to do well on the SAT? Learn how *ETS* operates and takes advantage of how *you* think.

ETS's Favorite Methods to Make Math Questions Difficult

1. Asking you to solve for unusual quantities
2. Nudging you to over-think or under-think a problem
3. Changing the order in which you're accustomed to solving a question
4. Stacking multiple concepts on top of one another
5. Referencing a concept without using its name or using a different name

---

As you work through this manual, remember that this test is designed to be more manipulative than difficult. Don't get angry or frustrated; work smarter, learn the techniques, and do better.

"If people knew how hard I worked to achieve my mastery, it wouldn't seem so wonderful after all."
- Michelangelo

Order of Difficulty

All Math questions on the SAT are organized by difficulty. None of the other questions on the test will be.

Question difficulty is tied directly to question number on the SAT. The higher the number, the more difficult the problem.

This doesn't seem very groundbreaking, but there are few important pieces of advice to take away.

These tips should help you make decisions more quickly when you're taking the test. There are only a handful of *legitimately* difficult math questions on the SAT. The rest are hard because you're falling for traps or misreading the questions.

1. All questions on the SAT are worth the same number of points.
2. Easy questions should have straightforward solutions.
3. Difficult questions should have thoughtful solutions.

Why You Should Care About Question Difficulty

Scenario #1

You're on number 3. You finished the question relatively quickly, but worry that you might be forgetting something or falling for a trick. What should you do?

(A)   Go back and check your work. Better safe than sorry.

(B)   Move on. If there's time left at the end, go back and check your work.

Scenario #2

You just finished number 38. You're feeling grateful because you know that #38 should be really difficult, but you got through it quickly. What should you do?

(A)   Go back and check your work. Better safe than sorry.

(B)   Move on. If there's time left at the end, go back and check your work.

Scenario #3

The proctor announces you have one minute left, but you have four unanswered questions in the section: #6, 12, 32, and 37. What should you do with the remaining minute?

(A)   Attempt the questions in numeric order. You're more likely to get the answer in the remaining time.

(B)   Scan the unanswered questions to find the one you're most likely to complete in the remaining time.

18

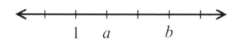

On the number line above, the tick marks are equally spaced. Which of the following expresses b in terms of a ?

A) $a + 2$

B) $2a + 2$

C) $3a - 2$

D) $3a$

Do you see how knowing the question difficulty can help you make the best decisions in each of these situations?

Scenario #1: B; Scenario #2: A; Scenario #3: B

19

Use the Question to Guide Your Approach

Try this:

1. Think of an integer between 20 and 30. _____
2. Find the sum of all the prime numbers less than the number you chose. _____
3. Subtract 1 from that sum. _____
4. Square the new number. _____
5. Find the product of the two smallest prime factors of that number. _____
6. Multiply that number by its inverse. (e.g., the inverse of 8 is $\frac{1}{8}$)

   What is the result? _____

Are you smacking yourself in the forehead right now? Any number times its inverse is always 1.

What's the point?

> 1. Read the ENTIRE question before you start your work.
> 2. Always write what you're solving for at the bottom of your workspace.
> 3. **Use the question itself** to guide how you approach the problem.

Reading the entire question and knowing what you're looking for will help you create the most effective solution strategy. Let's use an example you might see on the SAT.

9

If x and y are positive integers and $4^{2x}4^{2y} = 256$, what is the value of $x + y$?

A) 2
B) 4
C) 6
D) 8

RTFQ

DO NOT start solving a problem until you have read the question all the way through.

Stuck?

Set up your workspace like this:

9

If x and y are positive integers and $4^{2x}4^{2y} = 256$,
what is the value of $x + y$?

A) 2
B) 4
C) 6
D) 8

$4^{2X}4^{2Y} = 256$

$x + y =$

This simple action will tell you whether you're going in the right direction. Let's see how:

Add the exponents on the left:

$$4^{2x+2y} = 256$$

This must be the right first step because it's getting me closer to my goal. Let's work on the right side now by getting the bases the same:

$$4^{2x+2y} = 4^4$$

Since the bases are the same on both sides of the equation, you can set the exponents equal to each other.

$$2x + 2y = 4$$

Divide both sides by 2 and presto! You're done.

$$x + y = 2$$

Now try some on your own. Don't forget to set up your workspace. Like a boss.

12

If $\frac{5b}{2c} = \frac{8}{3}$, what is the value of $\frac{25b^2}{4c^2}$?

15

When the number p is multiplied by 5, the result is the same as when 5 is added to p. What is the value of $4p$?

A) $\frac{4}{5}$

B) $\frac{5}{4}$

C) 4

D) 5

13

If $\frac{(3a+b)}{b} = \frac{6}{5}$, what is the value of $\frac{a}{b}$?

16

A certain number m is multiplied by 11. The number that is 4 less than m is also multiplied by 11. How much greater is the first product than the second?

One more time…

- Your workspace should have the original equation(s) on top and what you're solving for at the bottom.
- For example, writing "x + y = " on the bottom of your workspace gives you a goal, ensures you're answering the question that's being asked, and forces you to consider the possibility that you will not be able to find x and y individually, but rather only as a collective quantity.

16

If $\frac{(3x+y)}{y} = \frac{4}{3}$, what is the value of $\frac{x}{y}$?

19

If $b = 3c$ and $a = 3$, what is the value of $ac - b$?

A) 0
B) 1
C) 3
D) 6

24

If $a = b - 1$, what is the value of $2a - 2b$?

A) -2
B) -1
C) 1
D) 2

21

If $3y - 2 \geq 1$, what is the least possible value of $3y + 2$?

A) 5
B) 3
C) 2
D) 1

23

If $\frac{3x}{2y} = \frac{9}{2}$, what is the value of $\frac{9x^2}{4y^2}$?

A) $\frac{9}{4}$
B) $\frac{18}{4}$
C) $\frac{18}{2}$
D) $\frac{81}{4}$

17

If $\sqrt{5} = x + 1$, what is the value of $(x + 1)^2$?

6

If $f(x) = -3x + 6$, what is $f(-2x)$ equal to?

A) $-6x - 4$
B) $6x + 4$
C) $6x + 6$
D) $6x^2 - 12x$

18

If $x = y + 2$, what is the value of $2x - 2y$?

23

Write it Out

Pencils are cheap. Use yours. Don't keep things in your head when you're working. Write it out. In fact, quite a few questions on the SAT can be solved with a *liberal* application of some organizational skills.

Consider the following question:

15

> A district has 15,000 registered voters, of which 60 percent are women and 40 percent are men. All the voters are either Democrat or Republican. If 4,500 of the voters are Republican and 2,500 of the Republican voters are women, how many of the voters are both male and Democrat?

There's quite a bit to keep track of. The best way to approach this problem is to create a grid:

	Women	Men	Total
Democrats			
Republicans			
Total			

Next, fill in the information provided in the problem:

	Women	Men	Total
Democrats			
Republicans	2,500		4,500
Total	9,000	6,000	15,000

Now, just fill in the missing fields by using the totals. If there are 4,500 total Republicans and 2,500 Republican women, finding the number of Republican men is easy. Continue that way for the remaining fields. Be sure to pay attention to what you're solving for!

liberal: adj., giving and generous in temperament or behavior

Piece of cake? You bet it is. Because you were organized. Nice work.

Other questions will feel more difficult than they actually are. If you just try writing it out, the situation will start to make more sense.

14

> The sum of nine different integers is zero. What is the least number of these integers that must be negative?

What happens when you start writing them out?

-7, -6, -5, -4, -3, -2, -1, 0, 1   Sum = -27

That doesn't work...

-4, -3, -2, -1, 0, 1, 2, 3, 4   Sum = 0

Well, that works. But... this is a number 14. It should be harder... Let me reread the question.

Oh. Duh. The numbers don't have to be consecutive, just different. Shift more numbers to the positive side and use bigger negative numbers...

-11, -6, -4, 1, 2, 3, 4, 5, 6   Sum = 0

That works, but I can do better...

-11, -10, 0, 1, 2, 3, 4, 5, 6   Sum = 0

Wow, I can user fewer positive numbers if I make them bigger. What if I take this to the extreme?

-36, 1, 2, 3, 4, 5, 6, 7, 8   Sum = 0

There it is!

 Get your pencil moving. It will help you make sense of the question.

25

18

16, 12, ...

In the sequence above, the first term is 16 and each term after the first is 4 more than half the previous term. What is the fifth term of the sequence?

32

The number p is the product of three different positive prime numbers greater than 2. If the sum of these three prime numbers is also prime, what is the smallest possible value for p ?

15

In a basketball league with 5 teams, each team plays exactly 2 games with each of the other 4 teams in the league. What is the total number of games played in this league?

16

On each of the days Monday through Friday, Arielle spent 1 hour walking to work and 1 hour walking back home. What fraction of the total number of hours in these five days did she spend commuting?

"All growth depends upon activity. There is no development physically or intellectually without effort, and effort means work."
- Calvin Coolidge

19

A social club plans to accept a total of 1,000 members for its new charter. Of the 800 members accepted so far, 60 percent are female and 40 percent are male. How many of the remaining members to be accepted must be male in order for half of the total number of members accepted to be male?

16

How many different ways are there to make 17 cents using only pennies, nickels, and dimes?

Longer word problems may seem to test your ability to determine what information is relevant. The SAT OCCASIONALLY provides extraneous information. It's not too common, though.

Draw It Out

This seems like pretty self-evident advice on Geometry questions that don't have a figure, but it goes beyond that. How could you use drawings on the following questions to help yourself reach the correct answer?

18

Six friends sit at a rectangular table with six seats, three on each of the long sides. Tim sits at the back right corner. Kate cannot sit next to Tim or directly opposite him. In how many different seats can Kate sit?

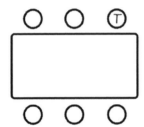

34

An electrician is testing 5 different wires. For each test, the electrician chooses 2 of the wires and connects them. What is the least number of tests that must be done so that every possible pair of wires is tested?

33

A container is 2/3 full of water. If 4 gallons of the water were removed from the container, it would be 1/2 full. How many gallons of water does this container hold when it is completely full?

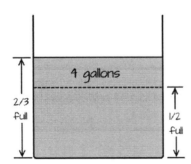

Your pencil is your best friend on the SAT.
Start small, write things out, and
DON'T KEEP EVERYTHING IN YOUR HEAD!

A good drawing can help you make observations that might have otherwise eluded you.

38

Five different points A, B, C, D, and E lie on a line in that order. The length of AD is 5.5 and the length of BE is 4.5. If the length of CD is 3, what is one possible value for the length of BC ?

16

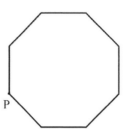

Point P is a vertex of an 8-sided polygon. The polygon has 8 sides of equal length and 8 angles of equal measure. When all possible diagonals are drawn from point P in the polygon, how many triangles are formed?

17

A cube has 2 faces painted black and the remaining faces painted white. The total area of the white faces is 36 square inches. What is the volume of the cube, in cubic inches?

A) 9
B) 27
C) 36
D) 48

18

The function f has the property that $f(r) = f(s)$ for all numbers r and s. What is the graph of $y = f(x)$ in the xy-plane?

A) A line with slope -1
B) A line with slope 0
C) A line with slope 1
D) A circle with center $(0, 0)$

Sometimes, it's a good idea to draw a picture based on the answer choices.

29

Translating English to Algebra

While there are ways around questions that contain difficult algebra, it's best to know how to translate a word problem into an algebraic expression that you can then simplify and solve.

Let's start with…

English Word(s)	Math Equivalent
increased by more than combined, together total of sum added to	**Addition** +
decreased by minus, less difference between/of less than, fewer than	**Subtraction** -
of times, multiplied by product of increased/decreased by a **factor**	**Multiplication** ×
per, a (e.g., 3 times a minute) out of ratio of, quotient of percent (divide by 100)	**Division** ÷
is, are, was, were, did, does, will be gives, yields sells for	**Equals** =
what a certain number a number	**Variable** (x, y, z…)

Try using these rules on the following questions.

16

If 7 less than twice a number is equal to 16, what is 4 times the number?

18

Admission tickets to a movie theater are $4.00 for a child and $8.00 for an adult. If 200 tickets were sold for a total of $1,400, what was the ratio of the number of children's tickets sold to the number of adults' tickets sold?

A) 1 to 4
B) 1 to 3
C) 1 to 2
D) 4 to 7

34

The sum of three numbers is 745. The first number is 50% more than the sum of the second and third numbers. What is the value of the first number?

37

A student spent a total of $9.60 for pens and pencils. Each pen costs 2 times as much as each pencil, and the customer bought 3 times as many pencils as pens. How much, in dollars, did the student spend on pens?

 The order of terms is important when you're dealing with subtraction or division.

On harder questions, you'll need a few more tools.

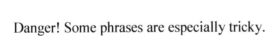

English Word(s)	Math Equivalent
consecutive integers	$x, x + 1, x + 2$, etc..
consecutive even integers	$x, x + 2, x + 4$, etc...
consecutive odd integers	$x, x + 2, x + 4$, etc...
square	x^2
square root	$\sqrt{x}$
cube	x^3
cube root	$\sqrt[3]{x}$
n percent of x	$\frac{n}{100}x$ or $\times.01nx$
x is increased by 20%	$x + .2x = 1.2x$
x is decreased by 20%	$x - .2x = .8x$
ratio of x to y	$\dfrac{x}{y}$

Danger! Some phrases are especially tricky.

If the problem says...	Don't do this...	Do this...
"There are three times as many x as y."	$3x = y$	$x = 3y$
"...five less than x"	$5 < x$ or $5 - x$	$x - 5$
"x is inversely related to y"	$\dfrac{x}{y} = c$	$xy = c$ or $x = \dfrac{c}{y}$
"x and y differ by less than 6"	$x - y < 6$ or $y - x < 6$	$\lvert x - y\rvert < 6$ or $-6 < x - y < 6$

Now try these questions.

4

If a, b, and c are positive numbers and the sum of a and b is equal to the square of c, which of the following is equivalent to c ?

A) $\sqrt{a} + \sqrt{b}$

B) $\sqrt{a + b}$

C) $\sqrt{a^2 + b^2}$

D) $a^2 + b^2$

18

A list consists of 11 consecutive integers. If the sum of the sixth and eleventh terms of the list is 31, what is the first term in this list?

17

If the length of a rectangle is increased by 20% and the width of the same rectangle is decreased by 20%, what is the ratio of the new area to the original area?

22

During a clothing sale, Joseph purchased a sweater at a 30 percent discount off its original price. The total amount he paid the cashier was d dollars, which included a 7 percent sales tax on the discounted price. Which of the following represents the original price of the sweater in terms of d ?

A) $0.77d$

B) $\dfrac{d}{0.77}$

C) $(0.7)(1.07)d$

D) $\dfrac{d}{(0.7)(1.07)}$

Use Definitions to Create Equations

Formulas are great. They really are. But they force us to think in a very specific way.

For instance, the formula for slope is

$$m = \frac{y_2 - y_1}{x_2 - x_1}$$

The implicit assumption with this formula is that we'll be given (x_1, y_1) and (x_2, y_2) to find m. So what happens when we get this problem?

17

Line l has a slope of $\frac{5}{4}$ and passed through points $(-4, 6)$ and $(3, t)$. What is the value of t?

Most people will draw a picture and begin counting up 5, over 4 until they hit the point they're looking for. They do this because they think the slope formula only works to find the slope.

Look at the formula again. Which values do we know?

$$\boldsymbol{m = \frac{y_2 - y_1}{x_2 - x_1}}$$

That's right: we have all but one of the variables. Find it.

$$\frac{5}{4} = \frac{t - 6}{3 - (-4)}$$

$$35 = 4(t - 6)$$

$$35 = 4t - 24$$

$$59 = 4t$$

$$14.75 = t$$

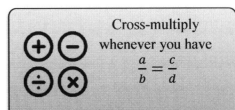

Cross-multiply whenever you have $\frac{a}{b} = \frac{c}{d}$

Don't limit yourself with formulas. If you have all but one of the variables, use the formula to create an equation that you can solve.

31

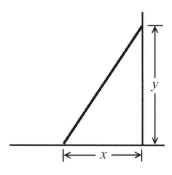

A ladder is extended from the ground to the side of a building as shown in the figure above. The ladder has a slope of $\frac{15}{8}$. If y is 7.5 feet, what is x, in feet?

32

A right angle is divided into three non-overlapping angles whose measures are $2w$, $3w$, and $5w$. What is the value of w?

33

In the xy-plane, the points with coordinates $(0, 1)$ and $(4, p)$ lie on line m. If the slope of m is greater than $\frac{3}{4}$ and less than 1, what is one possible value of p?

21

If the average (arithmetic mean) of y and $y + 2$ is a and if the average of y and $y - 2$ is b, what is the average of a and b?

A) $\frac{y}{2}$

B) y

C) $y + \frac{1}{2}$

D) $2y$

18

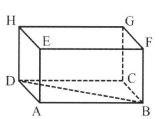

The volume of the rectangular solid above is 1152. If $AB = 6x$, $DB = 10x$, and $AE = 3x$, what is the value of x?

Thinking Mathematically

This is George Pólya.

He's the man. George had a lot of interesting insights into mathematical reasoning[1]. Here, we're going to condense a handful of his thoughts on problem solving generally and algebraic reasoning specifically.

If you're struggling with a math problem, consider the following steps.

1. Understand the Problem
   - Do you understand all the words used in stating the problem?
   - What are you asked to find or show?
   - Can you think of a picture or diagram that might help you understand the problem?
2. Devise a Plan
   - Guess and check
   - Make an orderly list
   - Eliminate possibilities
   - Use symmetry
   - Solve an equation
   - Look for a pattern
   - Draw a picture
   - Solve a simpler problem
   - Use a model
   - Work backwards
   - Use a formula
3. Carry out the Plan
4. Look Back

---

[1] If you'd like to learn more, check out *How To Solve It*, by George Pólya, 2nd ed., Princeton University Press, 1957.

Understand the Problem

Most of these suggestions are covered in other modules in this book (see the table at the end of this module to see the alignments), so we're going to focus on a few interesting examples here.

Solve a Simpler Problem

 37

A student spent a total of $9.60 for pens and pencils. Each pen costs 2 times as much as each pencil, and the customer bought 3 times as many pencils as pens. How much, in dollars, did the student spend on pens?

Stuck? Turn the page…

37

A student spent a total of $9.60 for pens and pencils. Each pen costs 2 times as much as each pencil, and the customer bought 3 times as many pencils as pens. How much, in dollars, did the student spend on pens?

unknowns

# of pens: a

# of pencils: b

cost of one pen: x

cost of one pencil: y

Amount spent on pens: ax

$x = 2y \qquad a = 3b$

$ax + by = 9.60$

$ax =$

Understand the Problem

What are the unknowns?

What am I being asked to find?

Devise a Plan

What would we do with unit price and quantity to determine the total amount spent?

Can't get it? What would be the charge for 15 gumballs that cost 4 cents each? How did you get that number?

When we can't generate a relationship between variables, try doing it with numbers to make it easier (just be careful with any unit conversions you do in your head).

Always pay attention to what you're being asked to solve for. RTFQ.

Given the two equations and your target quantity, can you figure out how to solve for ax ?

Use Symmetry

111, 117, 123…

The sequence above begins with 111. Each subsequent term is generated by adding six to the previous term. What is the sum of the first 14 terms of this sequence?

No calculators? Come on. Really?

Let's look and see how *symmetry* can help us find the answer.

25

111, 117, 123…

The sequence above begins with 111. Each subsequent term is generated by adding six to the previous term. What is the sum of the first 14 terms of this sequence?

111, 117, 123, 129...

14 terms is 13 changes from 111, so the final term is

111 + 6(13) = 189

Symmetry?

111, 117, 123, 129 … 171, 177, 183, 189

111 + 189 = 300
117 + 183 = 300
123 + 177 = 300
129 + 171 = 300

This can't be a coincidence...

14 terms means 7 pairs that each add up to 300.

7(300) = 2100

Boom.

We said it before, and we'll say it again: Pólya is the man. You'll find that a lot of his advice aligns nicely with several of the modules in this manual. If you'd like to learn more about a particular bit of advice, check out the corresponding module.

Pólya's Advice	Module Title
Understand all the words used in stating the problem.	*The Importance of Terminology*
Identify what you are asked to find or show.	*Use the Question to Guide Your Approach*
Use a formula	*Use Definitions to Create Equations*
Work backwards Eliminate possibilities Guess and check Solve a simpler problem	*Being Creative on Math*
Solve an equation	*Translating English to Algebra*
Look for a pattern	*Patterns and Sequences*
Think of a picture or diagram that might help you understand the problem Use a model Make an orderly list	*Write it Out*

Being Creative on Math Questions

There are at least two ways of dealing with many questions: you can solve algebraically or you can use your own numbers. We'll call these "The Algebra Approach" and "The Arithmetic Approach." You have to decide which one makes the most sense for you.

28

Let x and y be nonzero real numbers such that $2^{y+1} = 2x$. Which of the following is an expression for 2^{y+3} in terms of x ?

A) $\dfrac{1}{6x^3}$

B) $\dfrac{1}{4x}$

C) x^3

D) $8x$

Which approach do you prefer?

Algebra Approach

$$2^{y+1} = 2x$$

Multiply both sides by 2^2

$$2^2 2^{y+1} = 2x 2^2$$

$$2^{y+3} = 8x$$

Arithmetic Approach

Make up a value for y.

$$y = 3$$

Find x using the value you just made up.

$$2^{3+1} = 2x$$
$$x = 8$$

The question is asking for the value of 2^{y+3}. Find that.

$$2^{3+3} = 2^6 = 64$$

Evaluate each answer choice using $x = 8$ to find which one equals 64.

A) $\dfrac{1}{6x^3} = \dfrac{1}{6 \times 8^3} = \dfrac{1}{3072}$

B) $\dfrac{1}{4x} = \dfrac{1}{4 \times 8} = \dfrac{1}{32}$

C) $x^3 = 512$

D) $8x = 64$

It's important to swallow your pride here: choose the approach that's going to get you the right answer.

11

If $y = \frac{x}{4}$ and $x \neq 0$, what does $4x$ equal in terms of y?

A) $\frac{y}{4}$

B) $4y$

C) $8y$

D) $16y$

12

If the length of a rectangle is increased by 40% and the width of the same rectangle is decreased by 40%, what is the effect on the area of the rectangle?

A) It decreases by 16%

B) It remains the same

C) It increases by 16%

D) It increases by 20%

32

If x is a positive integer and $2^x + 2^{(x+1)} = n$, what is $2^{(x+2)}$ in terms of n?

A) n^2

B) $2n + 1$

C) $2n$

D) $\frac{4n}{3}$

16

A certain positive number p, which is greater than 4, is multiplied by 11. The number that is 4 less than p is also multiplied by 11. How much greater is the first product than the second?

How to Use Your Own Numbers

1. Identify the number that all the other numbers depend upon.
2. Pick a number that…
   a. satisfies any restrictions in the problem
   b. makes the math easy
   c. allows you to find the answer to the question
3. Find the answer to the question using the number you generated.
4. Eliminate Answer Choices that don't match your answer or pick the correct answer.

Or, you can try **Using Numbers in the Answer Choices.**

15

If $(a - b)^a = 1$ and $b^a = 1$, and a and b are both positive integers, what is the value of a ?

A) 1
B) 2
C) 3
D) 4

You know that a must equal 1, 2, 3, or 4. Pick one and try it out to see what happens.

Start with answer choice C).

$a = 3$

Start with the second statement.

if $b^3 = 1$, then $b = 1$

Check the first statement with the numbers you found.

$(3 - 1)^3 = 8$

8 doesn't equal 1

Eliminate answer choice C).

Check B).

$a = 2$
if $b^2 = 1$, $b = 1$
$(2 - 1)^2 = 1$

You got it! Choose B) and move on to the next question.

Using Numbers in the Answer Choices

1. Start with Answer Choice (C).
2. Work through the problem to determine whether (C) makes sense.
3. If (C) doesn't work, determine whether the number is too large or too small (if possible).
4. Move on to larger or smaller numbers in the answer choices until you find the number that produces a true statement.

7

When a certain even number is divided by 5, the remainder is 3. Which digit must be in the units place of this even number?

A) 0
B) 4
C) 6
D) 8

15

What is the least integer value of x for which
$\left|\frac{x}{3} - \frac{2}{3}\right| = \frac{x}{3} - \frac{2}{3}$?

A) 0
B) 1
C) 2
D) 3

13

$a^2 - b^2 < 6$
$a + b > 4$

If a and b are positive integers in the inequalities above, and $a > b$, what is the value of a ?

A) 1
B) 2
C) 3
D) 4

Working with Multiple Unknowns

There are going to be quite a few questions that will throw multiple unknown quantities at you. There are six strategies to keep in mind on these questions. Let's go through them one by one.

Solve for a Collective Quantity

Don't forget to RTFQ! If the question asks for the value of "x + y," don't try to find x and y.

Find "x + y."

8

If x and y are positive integers and $2^{2x}2^{2y} = 64$, what is the value of $x + y$?

A) 3
B) 4
C) 5
D) 6

18

If $3x - y = 8$, what is the value of $\frac{27^x}{3^y}$?

A) 3^8
B) 9^5
C) 27^3
D) The value cannot be determined from the information given.

16

If $4x + 8y - 8 = 10$, what is the value of $x + 2y$?

20

If $3x - 3 \geq 2$, what is the least possible value of $3x + 1$?

A) 6
B) 4
C) 2
D) 1

Use Substitution

If you can find the value of one of the unknowns, use that value to find the others. Or if you can express the value of the variable you want to eliminate in terms of a variable you want to stick around, use substitution.

24

A bag of trail mix consists of only raisins, pumpkin seeds, and peanuts. In the bag, the weights of the raisins and the pumpkin seeds are equal and the weight of the peanuts is twice the weight of the raisins. How many ounces of pumpkin seeds are there in 60 ounces of this trail mix?

A) 12
B) 15
C) 18
D) 21

28

The product of c and d is equal to x, and the sum of c and d is equal to y. If x and y are positive numbers, what is $\frac{1}{c} + \frac{1}{d}$ in terms of x and y?

A) $\frac{1}{x} + \frac{1}{y}$

B) xy

C) $\frac{y}{x}$

D) $\frac{x}{y}$

29

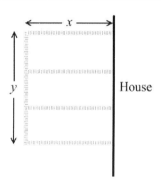

A garden has the dimensions x and y and a total area of 2,000 square feet. The garden is to be fenced off around the border and separated into three equal sections as indicated. In terms of y, how many feet of fencing is needed to bound the three sides of the garden and to create the three subdivisions?

A) $y + \frac{2,000}{y}$

B) $y + \frac{8,000}{y}$

C) $y + \frac{8,000}{3y}$

D) $3y + \frac{4,000}{3y}$

19

In a certain group of students, there are three times as many freshmen as sophomores and twice as many sophomores as juniors. If there are a total of 108 students, how many students are freshmen?

Stack, then Add or Subtract

If you can get the variables of two or more equations to line up, see if you can get something to drop out by adding or subtracting the equations. It helps if the coefficients are the same, so you might need to multiply one of the equations by a constant.

2

If $y - x = 5$ and $y + x = -15$, what is the value of y ?

A) -10
B) -5
C) 5
D) 10

12

If $ab = 4$, $ac = 8$, and $bc = 2$, and a, b, and c are positive, what is the value of abc ?

A) 8
B) 16
C) 32
D) 64

8

$$4x + 6y = -20$$
$$3y - x = -13$$

What is the solution (x, y) to the system of equations above?

A) $(16, 1)$
B) $(1, -4)$
C) $(-2, -2)$
D) $(10, -3)$

22

$$d = b - c + 4$$
$$d = c - a - 3$$
$$d = a - b + 5$$

Based on the system of equations above, what is the value of d ?

A) 2
B) 3
C) 4
D) 6

If adding or subtracting the equations isn't working, what other operation could you use?

Hint: It starts with an "m" and rhymes with *schmultiplication.*

Wait for an Unknown to Drop Out

The nice thing about equations is that if you have the same thing on both sides of the equal sign, you can get it to drop out:

$$2x + 6 + k = 4x + 14 + k \quad \rightarrow \quad 2x + 6 = 4x + 14$$

This works with division, too.

32

During a 100-minute period, the number of bacteria in a Petri dish could be modeled by the function $p(t) = \frac{t^2}{2} - 20t + c$. In the function, c is a constant and p(t) represents the population on minute t for $0 \leq t \leq 99$. On what minute was the number of bacteria in the Petri dish the same as it was on minute number 10?

19

On his way to school, Billy walks on pavement $\frac{3}{5}$ of the time and on grass $\frac{2}{5}$ of the time. His pavement walking rate is 4 miles per hour, and his grass walking rate is 2 miles per hour. The distance that Billy walks on grass is what fraction of the total distance he walked to school?

Use Your Own Number or a Number in the Answer Choices

Our old friends. Don't forget about these two strategies!

16

If $10^{xy} = 10{,}000$, where x and y are positive integers, what is one possible value of x ?

20

On his way to school, Billy walks on pavement $\frac{3}{5}$ of the time and on grass $\frac{2}{5}$ of the time. His pavement walking rate is 4 miles per hour, and his grass walking rate is 2 miles per hour. The distance that Billy walks in grass is what fraction of the total distance he walked to school?

28

If $ab = 4$, $ac = 8$, and $bc = 2$, and a, b, and c are positive, what is the value of abc ?

A) 8
B) 16
C) 32
D) 64

31

If x is the average (arithmetic mean) of n and 6, b is the average of $4n$ and 13, and c is the average of $2n$ and 11, what is the average of a, b, and c in terms of n ?

A) $n + 5$
B) $n + 6$
C) $3n + 15$
D) $6n + 30$

Use a Single Variable

Why use an x and a y to represent two unknown quantities when you can get away with just an x? If there's a straightforward relationship between two or more unknown quantities, see if you can represent them all in terms of one variable.

6

Last winter Asha ate 17 more acorns than Theon. They ate a combined total of 71 acorns, how many acorns did Asha eat last winter?

A) 27
B) 35
C) 37
D) 44

31

The first of three numbers is 4 times the second number. The third number is 40 more than the second number. If the sum of all three numbers is 154, what is the value of the first number?

14

Cari has 19 tokens that she earned in a game of chance. All of the tokens are worth 4 points each or 5 points each. The total value of all of her tokens is exactly 84 points. How many 5-point tokens does Cari have?

A) 5
B) 6
C) 7
D) 8

34

At a pizzeria, a slice of pizza costs $1.25 more than a soda. If a couple orders 3 slices of pizza and 2 sodas for a total of $9.50, how much does one slice of pizza cost? (Assume no sales tax is included)

Summary

Method	# of Equations Needed
Solve for a Collective Quantity	One or more
Use Substitution	Two or more
Stack, then Add or Subtract	Two or more
Wait for an Unknown to Drop Out	One or more
Use Your Own Number or Number in the Answer Choices	One or more
Use a Single Variable	One or more

Inequalities

For the most part, you can treat inequalities the same way you would normal equations.

Example:

If $3x + 5 > x + 2$, what is x ?

$$3x + 5 = x + 2 \qquad \leftarrow \text{Change the} > \text{into a} =$$

$$2x = -3 \qquad \leftarrow \text{Combine like terms}$$

$$x = 3/2 \qquad \leftarrow \text{Solve for x}$$

$$x > 3/2 \qquad \leftarrow \text{Change the} = \text{back into a} >$$

Simple.

Don't get confused by wording that essentially means "solve for x."

11

$-2 \leq 4x - 7$

Which of the following represents all values of x that satisfy the inequality above?

A) $x \geq \frac{5}{4}$

B) $x \leq \frac{5}{4}$

C) $x \geq -\frac{5}{4}$

D) $x \leq -\frac{4}{5}$

13

Which of the following graphs represents the set of all x values for which $-3 \leq x - 6 \leq 2$?

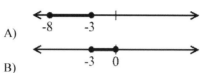

A)

B)

C)

D)

The only exception to the advice above is when you multiply or divide the entire inequality by a negative number. Then you have to flip the sign.

Example:

$-2x + 5 > 15$
$-2x > 10$
$x < -5$

Things can get a little more difficult when you're dealing with exponents.

Example:

$2x^2 > 32$
$x^2 > 16$
$x > 4 \; or \; x < -4$

Lastly, inequalities with absolute values pop up every once in a while and require an extra step.

Example: **Steps:**

$|x - 40| < 10$
$x - 40 < 10 \; and \; x - 40 > -10$ ←Split the inequality into two separate inequalities
$x < 50 \; and \; x > 30$ ←Solve each inequality separately

6

If $|5 - 4y| > 19$, which of the following is a possible value of y?

A) 4
B) 5
C) 6
D) 7

22

A decibel (dB) is a unit of sound loudness. A comfortable listening level for a home stereo system is between 50dB and 80dB. If x represents the dB level of a sound, which inequality expresses all comfortable listening levels?

A) $|x - 50| < 30$
B) $|x - 65| < 15$
C) $|x - 75| < 30$
D) $|x - 75| < 15$

Negative Numbers

Negative numbers pop up all over the place on the SAT. Most of the questions rely on your knowledge of negative number trivia, so let's review the basics.

Negative Number Trivia

Addition and Subtraction: $x + (-y) = x - y$ and $x - (-y) = x + y$

Multiplication: $x(-y) = -xy$ and $-x(-y) = xy$

Division: $\dfrac{x}{-y} = -\dfrac{x}{y}$ and $\dfrac{-x}{-y} = \dfrac{x}{y}$

Exponents: $(-x)^2 = x^2$ and $(-x)^3 = -x^3$

Roots: $\sqrt{16} = +4\ only$ and $\sqrt[3]{-27} = -3$

Absolute Value: $|-x| = x$ and $|x| = 2 \rightarrow x = \pm 2$

Reminders:
Fractions between -1 and 0 get *bigger* when you raise them to a power.
Fractions between 0 and 1 get *smaller* when you raise them to a power.
Fractions between 0 and 1 get *bigger* when you take a root.
$x + (-x) = 0$

On a number line, negative numbers go *left*.

A negative number raised to an *even* power will be *positive*. $(-2)^2 = 4$
A negative number raised to an *odd* power will be *negative*. $(-2)^3 = -8$

These pieces of trivia will get you through almost any problems involving negative numbers.

9

If $(n - 2)^2 = 36$ and $n < 0$, what is the value of n ?

A) -34
B) -8
C) -4
D) -2

13

The sum of nine different integers is zero. What is the least number of these integers that must be positive?

12

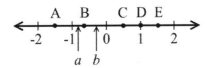

Which of the lettered points on the number line above corresponds to the value of the product ab ?

A) A
B) B
C) C
D) D

Fractions

Humanity went *millennia* without using fractions. We didn't think of counting less than one of something.

Fortunately, fractions came along and freed us from the tyranny of 1. We could count by units smaller than one. That's all fractions are.

The confusion comes when you have to work with different counting preferences (denominators), say, counting by $\frac{1}{2}$ or $\frac{3}{7}$. Basic operations and conceptualization become more complicated.

Addition and Subtraction

Make the denominators the same or use the bowtie method.

$$\frac{3}{4} + \frac{5}{7} = \frac{21}{28} + \frac{20}{28} = \frac{41}{28} \quad \text{or} \quad \overset{21}{\frac{3}{4}} \times \overset{20}{\frac{5}{7}} = \frac{41}{28}$$

Multiplication

Multiply straight across.

$$\frac{2}{9} \times \frac{5}{13} = \frac{10}{117}$$

Division

Flip the divisor and multiply.

$$\frac{\frac{4}{5}}{\frac{2}{3}} = \frac{4}{5} \times \frac{3}{2} = \frac{12}{10} = \frac{6}{5}$$

Follow these steps every time and you will avoid making needless mistakes. Oh, and your calculator is your best friend here. Just don't forget to use those parentheses!

Drawing a picture can be very helpful.

19

A container is 2/3 full of water. If 4 gallons of the water were removed from the container, it would be 1/2 full. How many gallons of water does this container hold when it is completely full?

11

If $\frac{2}{x} = 200$, what is the value of $x + \frac{1}{x}$?

A) 100.01
B) 100.2
C) 200.01
D) 200.1

16

A construction manager has 90 hours budgeted for projects A, B, and C. If $\frac{1}{3}$ of this time is used for project A and $\frac{3}{4}$ of the remaining time is used for project B, how many hours does the manager have left for project C ?

17

If $\frac{3a+b}{b} = \frac{7}{6}$, what is the value of $\frac{a}{b}$?

Proportions

$$\frac{2x}{5} = \frac{7}{16}$$

Cross multiply and solve.

$$32x = 35$$

$$x = \frac{35}{32}$$

Percents

Percents are just fractions in disguise.

Percents are a very specific type of fraction: one in which the denominator is always 100.

The key is translating percent verbiage into a solvable equation. For that, you need to know these four words.

English	Algebraic Equivalent
"percent" or "%"	$\dfrac{}{100}$
"what"	unknown (x, y, etc…)
"of"	multiply ($\times$)
"is", "are", "were", "did", "does"	$=$

Now that you know the language of percents, try a few questions. Just do a word-for-word translation from English to Math.

Example

What number is 25% of 75% of 250 ?

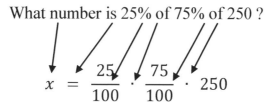

$$x = \frac{25}{100} \cdot \frac{75}{100} \cdot 250$$

16

What is $\frac{1}{2}$ of 26 percent of 550 ?

14

A rectangle is to be altered by increasing its length by 20 percent and decreasing its width by 20 percent. What effect will this have on the area of the rectangle?

A) It will decrease by 10%.
B) It will decrease by 4%.
C) It will increase by 4%.
D) It will increase by 10%

17

In a certain election, 40 percent of those who voted were females. If 4,200 males voted, what was the total number of people who voted in the election?

19

A salesperson's commission is p percent of the selling price of the condo. Which of the following represents the commission, in dollars, on 2 condos that sold for $35,000 each?

A) $700p$
B) $70,000p$
C) $\frac{35,000}{100+2p}$
D) $\frac{70,000+p}{100}$

If you're stuck, don't forget other strategies. Your own number, perhaps?

Exponents

Ah, the dreaded little number that makes other numbers big. Let's start with the basics when the bases are the same:

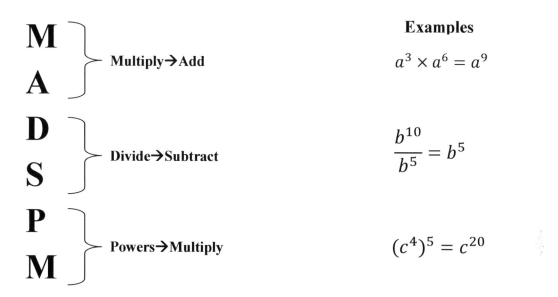

M
A } Multiply→Add

D
S } Divide→Subtract

P
M } Powers→Multiply

Examples

$$a^3 \times a^6 = a^9$$

$$\frac{b^{10}}{b^5} = b^5$$

$$(c^4)^5 = c^{20}$$

 Think "**Mad Spam**." This mnemonic will get you through a handful of basic exponent questions. Try a few.

A few pieces of trivia are sometime very helpful.

$w^0 = 1$ $\qquad\qquad\qquad\qquad$ $5{,}214^0 = 1$

$x^1 = x$ $\qquad\qquad\qquad\qquad$ $2536^1 = 2536$

$y^{-a} = \dfrac{1}{y^a}$ $\qquad\qquad\qquad$ $4^{-3} = \dfrac{1}{4^3} = \dfrac{1}{64}$

$z^{\frac{b}{c}} = \sqrt[c]{z^b}$ or $(\sqrt[c]{z})^b$ $\qquad$ $27^{\frac{2}{3}} = \sqrt[3]{27^2}$ or $(\sqrt[3]{27})^2 = 9$

$0^n = 0$ $\qquad\qquad\qquad\qquad$ $0^{1{,}412{,}522} = 0$

12

If $a^5 = 50$ and $b^2 = 10$, what is the value of $a^{10}b^{-2}$?

A)   5
B)   25
C)   50
D)   250

25

$(x + 4)^2 = 0$

How many different values of x satisfy the equation above?

A)   0
B)   1
C)   2
D)   3

14

If $x = y^3$ for any positive integer y, and if $z = x^2 + x$, what is z in terms of y ?

A) $y^3 + y$
B) $y^5 + y^3$
C) $y^6 + y$
D) $y^6 + y^3$

18

If $x^{\frac{y}{3}} = 27$ for positive integers x and y, what is one possible value of y ?

And every once in a while, you'll have to do a little gymnastics with the bases. Use this problem as a guide:

Example

$16^{3x} = 2^{36}$ Yikes.

$(2^4)^{3x} = 2^{36}$ Transform the left side of the equation to get the bases the same.

$2^{12x} = 2^{36}$ Follow rules of exponents.

$12x = 36$ If the bases are the same, you can equate the exponents.

$x = 3$ Voila!

16

If $10^{ab} = 100{,}000$, where a and b are positive integers, what is one possible value of a ?

18

17. If $\frac{36^a}{27^{4b}} = 9^{21}$, what is the value of $a - 2b$?

17

If a and b are positive integers and $3^{2a}9^b = 81$, what is the value of $a + b$?

Absolute Value

Absolute Value will pop up once or twice per test. The *customary* definition – distance from zero – will get you through most questions.

6

On a number line, the number t is halfway between 1 and 2. What is the value of $|1 - t|$?

A) $-\frac{3}{2}$

B) $-\frac{1}{2}$

C) $\frac{1}{2}$

D) $\frac{5}{2}$

16

$$|x - 2| = \frac{1}{4}$$

What is the least value of x that satisfies the equation above?

  Remember, equations with absolute values generally have two solutions. Generate two equations and solve them individually.

$$|c + 5| = 4 \quad \rightarrow \quad c + 5 = 4 \quad and \quad c + 5 = -4$$

Things can get a bit more complicated when the SAT throws in inequalities or exponents (check out the Inequalities Module for more info). Deal with the positive and negative values separately.

3

If $|6 - 5x| > 30$, which of the following is a possible value of x ?

A) 5
B) 6
C) 7
D) 8

16

$$f(x) = |3x - 17|$$

For the function defined above, what is one possible value of a for which $f(a) < a$?

Lastly, you might have to deal with absolute values and graphs. Just think of the x-axis value as a mirror: anything that dips below the x-axis gets reflected up.

17

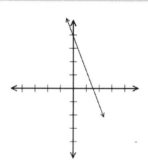

The equation of the line above is $y = -3x + 4$. Which of the following is the graph of $y = |-3x + 4|$?

B)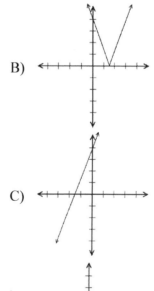

C)

A)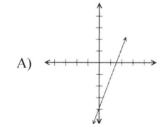

D)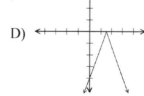

Remainders

The SAT will occasionally ask you about remainders. As with other question types, they'll make the items more difficult by changing up the order. The test will often give you the remainder, so knowing where the remainder comes from is important.

Finding Remainders and Additional Dividends

Example

$27 \div 6 = 4\,r3$ because the closest multiple of 6 to 27 is 24, which is 3 shy of 27.

What other numbers would produce a remainder of 3 when divided by 6 ?

 15, 33, 39, 51, 69, etc…

Notice anything about these numbers?

They're all exactly 3 (the remainder identified above) more than multiples of our divisor (6).

Make sense? You have probably realized by now that calculators aren't super helpful when finding remainders. Use your long division, children.

16

When the positive integer p is divided by 9, the remainder is 8. What is the remainder when $p + 2$ is divided by 9 ?

21

When the positive integer a is divided by 14, the remainder is 4. When the positive integer b is divided by 14, the remainder is 5. What is the remainder when the product ab is divided by 7 ?

A) 3
B) 4
C) 5
D) 6

17

When the positive integer a is divided by 9, the remainder is 6. When the positive integer b is divided by 9, the remainder is 3. What is the remainder when the product ab is divided by 6 ?

Remember when we said your calculator isn't the best thing to use on remainder questions? We stand by that. But if you really want to know how to find a remainder with your calculator, here goes:

1. Divide your dividend by your divisor. $390 \div 16 = 24.375$
2. Chop off the decimal portion of the result. $24.375 \rightarrow .375$
3. Multiply the decimal by your original divisor. $.375 \times 16 = 6$
4. That's your remainder! (you might have to round a bit if you get a very ugly decimal in step 1)

Pro Tip: If your calculator can do mixed numbers, you can find the remainder easily. It is the numerator of the fraction.

Factors and Multiples

A **factor** of a number is an integer that goes evenly into that number.

Example: The positive factors of 60 are 1, 2, 3, 4, 5, 6, 12, 15, 20, 30, and 60.

Important Factors Reminders

- A number is **always** a factor of itself.
- 1 is **always** a factor of an integer.
- If a question doesn't explicitly refer to positive factors, you **must** consider negative factors as well.
- An integer will **always** have a *finite* number of factors.

A **multiple** of a number is what you would land on if you were counting by that number.

Example: Multiples of 60 are …-120, -60, 0, 60, 120, 180…

Important Multiple Reminders

- A number is **always** a multiple of itself.
- 0 is **always** a multiple of an integer.
- If a question doesn't explicitly refer to positive multiples, you **must** consider zero and negative multiples as well.
- An integer will **always** have an *infinite* number of multiples.

17

What is one possible three-digit positive integer that satisfies all of the following conditions?

- Each digit is different factor of 30.
- The integer is even.
- The sum of the digits is 11.

18

How many positive integers less than 1000 are not divisible by 6 ?

23

If x, y, and z are different positive integers such that x is divisible by y, and y is divisible by z, which of the following statements must be true?

    I. x is divisible by z.

    II. x has at least 3 positive factors.

    III. $x = yz$

A) I only
B) I and II only
C) I and III only
D) I, II, and III

Proportions (Variation)

Proportions come in two varieties: direct and indirect (inverse). We'll handle them separately.

Direct Proportion (Direct Variation)

With Direct Proportions, $\dfrac{x}{y}$ is always the same. If x gets bigger, y has to get bigger, or if x gets smaller, y gets smaller. In either case the **quotient** is the same.

$$\dfrac{x_1}{y_1} = \dfrac{x_2}{y_2} \quad \text{or} \quad \dfrac{x}{y} = k, \text{where } k \text{ is a constant}$$

16

A recipe requires $1\frac{2}{3}$ cups of cherry juice for 3 gallons of punch. At this rate, how many cups of cherry juice should be used for 5 gallons of punch?

9

At a copy store, the total cost to make 30 copies is d dollars. At this rate, what is the total cost, in dollars, to make 50 copies, in terms of d?

A) $\frac{3}{5}d$

B) $\frac{2}{3}d$

C) $\frac{3}{2}d$

D) $\frac{5}{3}d$

Sometimes the test won't use the words "proportion" or "varies directly." These questions will include situations involving rate, work, maps, or packaging.

Inverse Proportion (Inverse Variation)

Inverse variation is different because the **product** of x and y is a constant. As x gets bigger, y must get smaller to produce the same product. This *almost never* comes up on the test.

$$x_1 y_1 = x_2 y_2 \text{ or } xy = k, where\ k\ is\ a\ constant$$

12

Which of the following functions possesses an inverse relationship between x and $f(x)$?

A)

x	f(x)
2	3
4	6
6	9
8	12
10	15

B)

x	f(x)
2	15
4	12
6	9
8	6
10	3

C)

x	f(x)
2	30
4	15
6	10
8	7.5
10	6

D)

x	f(x)
2	10
4	8
6	6
8	4
10	2

Ratios

Ratios can be pretty scary for many students. Luckily, they don't appear very frequently on the SAT. If you get a ratio question, just think about how much you like drinking punch.

Your favorite punch is 2 parts orange juice to 3 parts cherry juice. How many cups of each do you need to make 15 cups of perfect punch?

Remember, the 2:3 ratio is a recipe. Since this question is asking about cups, let's pretend the recipe calls for 2 cups of orange juice to every 3 of cherry juice. How many cups of punch does that give you?

Orange	Cherry	Total
2	3	5

How many cups of punch do you need?

Orange	Cherry	Total
2	3	5
		15

So by what factor do you need to multiply the recipe?

Orange	Cherry	Total
2	3	5
3	3	3
		15

Since you're tripling the recipe, how many cups of orange and cherry juices do you need?

You can double-check your work by adding the numbers. Do they add up to the total? Yep. Move on.

	1st part of ratio	2nd part of ratio	total
ratio			
multiplier			
actual numbers			

4

In a social club, the ratio of men to women is 2:3. If there are 60 people in the social club, how many men are there?

A) 20
B) 24
C) 30
D) 40

17

A certain type of steel is made by combining iron and carbon so that the ratio of iron to carbon is 19 to 1 by weight. How many pounds of iron are needed to make a 380-pound anvil from this type of steel?

14

In a day care center, the ratio of caretakers to children is 1:4. Which of the following numbers CANNOT represent the total number of people at the day care center?

A) 20
B) 24
C) 25
D) 40

Patterns and Sequences

Sequence questions come in a few flavors. Most rely on scare tactics: If the problem asks for the 83rd term, it's natural to think to yourself, "How the heck am I going to write out 83 terms in time?"

The trick to answering these types of questions is finding a pattern or shortcut that will make your life easier. Write enough to find the *pattern*, then work from there.

Pattern Example

The Black Eyed Peas have a new song that goes "Red, Green, Blue, Yellow, Orange, Purple, Black, Red, Green, Blue, Yellow, Orange, Purple, Black…" as part of an experiment to determine how bad music has to be before people refuse to listen to it. If the song starts on "Red", what color is the 82nd color they sing?

Calendar Method

R	G	Be	Y	O	P	Bk
1	2	3	4	5	6	7
8	9	10	11	12	13	14
15	16	17	18	19	20	21
				82	83	84

Division Method

$$82 \div 7 = 11\,r5$$

The remainder is 5, so the answer is the fifth term.

5

16, 10, ...

In the sequence above, the first term is 16 and each term after the first is 2 more than half the previous term. What is the fifth term of the sequence?

A) 4.75
B) 5
C) 5.5
D) 7

17

50, 2, 50, 4, ...

In the sequence above, all odd-numbered terms beginning with the first term are 50. The even-numbered terms are the consecutive positive even integers. What is the difference between the 51st and the 50th term?

7

Starting with a red marble, colored beads are placed on a string according to the pattern red, pink, blue, yellow, white, orange, and black. If this pattern is repeated, what is the color of the 51st bead?

A) red
B) pink
C) blue
D) yellow

23

4, x, y, 4, ...

In the sequence above, the first term is 4 and the second term is x. Each term after the second is the product of the two immediately preceding terms. If $x < 0$, what is the 10th term of the sequence?

A) -4^{21}
B) -4^{10}
C) 4^{10}
D) 4^{21}

Sometimes, you can go straight to the answer choices if you know the formulas for arithmetic and geometric sequences...

Arithmetic Sequences (every term is d greater than the previous one)

$$a_n = a_1 + (n-1)d$$

a_n: nth term
a_1: first term
n: term number
d: difference

Example: If the first term of a sequence is 7, each term is 4 greater than the previous one, and we're looking for the 21st term, the formula will look like this:

$$a_{21} = 7 + (21 - 1)4$$
$$a_{21} = 7 + 80$$
$$a_{21} = 87$$

Geometric Sequences (every term is r times the previous one)

$$a_n = a_1 r^{n-1}$$

a_n: nth term
a_1: first term
n: term number
r: multiplier

Example: If the first term of a sequence is 3, each term is 4 times the previous one, and we're looking for the 7th term, the formula will look like this:

$$a_{12} = 3 \times 4^{7-1}$$
$$a_{12} = 3 \times 4096$$
$$a_{12} = 12,288$$

Count the Intervals

Some people dread figuring out how many days away an event is or how long something will take. People who are otherwise totally *competent* will insist on counting on their fingers when it comes to this stuff.

Why?

Well, consider the following question:

If at 2:00PM I have 7 jellybeans and eat one every half an hour, at what time will I eat the last one?

The obvious approach would be to divide 7 by two (or multiply by ½) to get 3 ½, which we add to 2:00PM to get 5:30. However, what would happen if we drew it out?

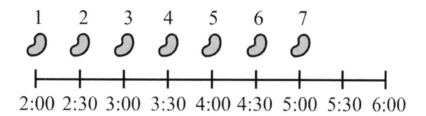

Seven jellybeans will only last **three** hours.

We make this mistake because when we count things, we start at 1. However, these types of scenarios actually have you starting at 0. Small – but important – difference.

You can avoid making these mistakes in the future by determining the relationship between the dividers (in this case, jelly beans) and the number of spaces (half hour intervals). Drawing it out can help a great deal.

competent: adj., having suitable or sufficient skill, knowledge, experience, etc., for some purpose; properly qualified

Let's try it on a real SAT question.

15

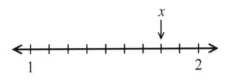

On the number line above, the tick marks are equally spaced. What is the value of the tick mark with x ?

17

Each term of a certain sequence is greater than the term before it. The difference between any two consecutive terms in the sequence is always the same number. If the fourth and seventh terms of the sequence are 13 and 73, respectively, what is the ninth term?

18

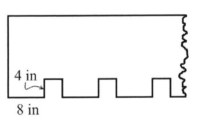

One end of a 120-inch-long curtain is shown in the figure above. The notched edge, shown in bold, was formed by removing a square from the end of each 8-inch length on one edge of the fabric. What is the total length, in inches, of the notched edge on the 120-inch curtain?

16

In a sequence, each term after the first is found by adding the constant c to the preceding term. The 10th term in the sequence is 13, and the 16th term is 31. What is the 7th term in the sequence?

A) 5
B) 6
C) 7
D) 8

Remember: Focus on finding the number of gaps or intervals.

Permutations and Combinations

How many different versions of something are possible given certain options? These types of questions strike fear into the hearts of students everywhere. There are a few different ways to tackle them, and the approach you choose will depend on what type of question you're dealing with.

Good news: these questions are exceedingly rare. Chances are high you won't even see one.

Let's go through the different varieties:

Count it Out

If the answer choices are relatively small numbers or there are too many rules to make a systematic solution, just write it out. If you do, BE ORGANIZED.

17

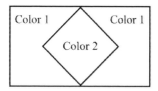

A designer is creating a flag in the figure above. If six colors are available for the design and color 1 cannot be the same as color 2, how many different color combinations can the designer choose from?

18

Any 2 points determine a line. If there are 5 points in a plane, no 3 of which lie on the same line, how many lines are determined by pairs of these 5 points?

Permutations

Permutations can be thought of as arrangements (e.g., "I have five trophies and want to put them all on my mantle. In how many ways can I display my awesomeness?") They're way more common than combinations, so we'll focus on them. The key to solving permutation problems is focusing on a) the number of decisions you have to make and b) the number of options you have for each of those decisions.

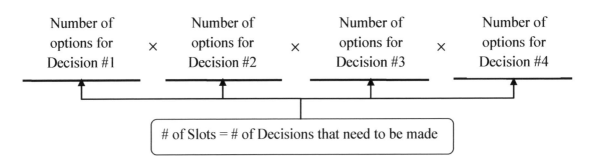

Permutations

18

Arielle has a red shirt, a green shirt, and a yellow shirt. She also has three jackets - one red, one green, and one yellow - and three pairs of pants - one red, one green, and one yellow. Arielle wants to wear a red, green, and yellow outfit consisting of one shirt, one jacket, and one pair of pants. How many different possibilities does she have?

Combinations

Combination questions ask how many groups can be made. Think about forming a basketball team – Albert, Benny, Charlie, Dwayne, and Ephram is the same team as Ephram, Dwayne, Charlie, Benny, and Albert. Combination questions are exceedingly rare on the SAT. It's very unlikely you'll see one on the test.

You can treat them exactly like permutations. The only difference is you have to get rid of the duplicates at the end of process.

Combinations

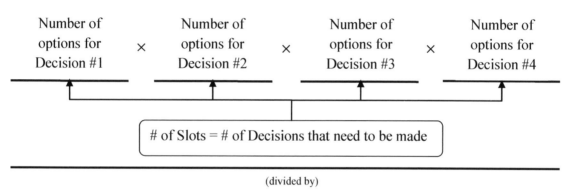

| Number of options for Decision #1 | × | Number of options for Decision #2 | × | Number of options for Decision #3 | × | Number of options for Decision #4 |

# of Slots = # of Decisions that need to be made

(divided by)

(# of Slots)!

19

A phone operator is testing 6 different ports. For each test, the operator chooses 2 of the ports and connects them with a wire. What is the least number of tests that must be done so that every possible pair of ports is tested?

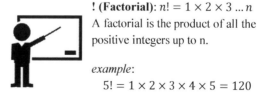

! **(Factorial)**: $n! = 1 \times 2 \times 3 \dots n$
A factorial is the product of all the positive integers up to n.

example:
$5! = 1 \times 2 \times 3 \times 4 \times 5 = 120$

The Number Line

While the number line is ostensibly straightforward, ETS has a few dirty tricks it likes to use. These tricks prey upon your *aversion* to counting by anything other than 1 or powers of ten.

16

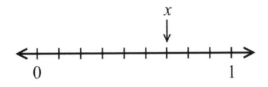

In the figure above, tick marks are equally spaced on the number line. What is the value of x?

10

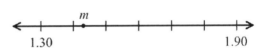

On the number line above, which has equally spaced tick marks, *m* could be equivalent to which of the following fractions?

A) $\frac{4}{3}$

B) $\frac{7}{6}$

C) $\frac{7}{5}$

D) $\frac{13}{9}$

aversion: noun, a strong feeling of dislike, opposition, repugnance, or antipathy

The key is to count the number of spaces.
DO NOT focus only on the endpoints or the number of hash marks.

11

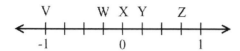

Tick marks are equally spaced on the number line above. Which of the lettered points has a coordinate equal to $-\left(\frac{1}{2}\right)^2$?

A) V
B) W
C) X
D) Y

24

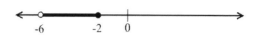

Which of the following inequalities represents the graph above?

A) $-6 < x + 2 \le -2$
B) $-6 \le x + 2 < -2$
C) $-4 < x + 2 \le 0$
D) $-4 \le x + 2 < 0$

Sometimes, you'll be asked to plot the results of an inequality on a number line. Remember that open circles are for < and > and closed circles are for ≤ and ≥.

Exponential Growth and Decay

You already know how to increase a number by a certain percentage:

"When n is increased by 23%, it is equal to 72% of q." → $1.23n = .72q$

Piece of cake, right?

But what if you want to increase (or decrease) a number by a certain percentage multiple times?

21

A bank account accumulates 4% compounded annually. Rounded to the nearest dollar, how much will a $150 deposit be worth after 10 years?

After 1 year: 150(1.04) = $156
After 2 years: 156(1.04) = $162.24
After 3 years: 162.24(1.04) = $168.7296
After 4 years: $168.7296(1.04) = $175.478784
After 5 years: FML

Not pretty. Perhaps a formula can save the day.

$$T = P(1 \pm r)^n$$

Where...

T:	final amount
P:	initial amount
r:	interest rate (positive for growth, negative for decay)
n:	number of iterations

So for the problem above...

T = 150(1 + .04)^{10} = 222.03
Piece of cake.

13

Nick purchases a share of a company's stock for $240. Experts expect the stock to increase in value by 7% every year for the next five years. If the predictions are correct, what will be the value, to the nearest dollar, of Nick's stock at the end of the five-year period?

A) 324
B) 330
C) 337
D) 354

17

Of the following four population growth models, which option would result in an exponential growth in a particular population?

A) Every year, 3% of the initial population is added to the population.
B) Every year, 2% of the initial population and 40 people are added to the population.
C) Every year, 1% of the current population is added to population.
D) Every year, 50 people are added to the population.

Questions 34 and 35 refer to the following information.

Sociologists are studying a village that is experiencing an annual 2% decrease in its population. The village's population currently is 5,000 people. The sociologists use the expression $5{,}000(r)^t$ to predict the population after t years.

34

What is the value of r in the expression above?

35

The sociologists discovered another village whose population is decreasing at a rate of 5% annually. This village currently has a population of 5,000. If the populations of both villages continue to decline at their respective current rates, how many more people will the first village have than the second? (Round your answer to the nearest integer when gridding your response.)

Geometry Introduction

Geometry on the SAT can be tough for two reasons:

1. You haven't done it in a while and are likely a bit rusty.
2. The questions can be frustratingly open-ended. Where do you start?

Getting better at Geometry questions will involve developing two skills:

1. Learn what rules/facts/formulas you'll need to know for the test.
2. Have a reliable strategy that will always point you in the right direction.

Follow this approach on every single geometry question.

1. Get all information from the question onto the figure.
    a. No figure? Draw one.
    b. Figure not drawn to scale? Redraw it or be VERY careful.
2. Info Dump
    a. What are relevant formulas? Write them down.
    b. What are relevant facts? Write them down.
3. Relate the provided info to the objective.
    a. Determine which formula is helpful.
    b. Determine which facts get you from the question to the answer.
4. If you're still not there, get creative! (optional)
    a. Estimate
    b. Use Your Own Numbers

 Remember: What the **FIRC**?

Figure → **I**nfo Dump →

Relate Question to Answer → Get **C**reative

Geometry Fact Sheet

On Geometry questions, there are some things you just need to know. Memorize this list of geometry facts:

Plane Geometry

Lines

There are 180 degrees in a *straight line*.

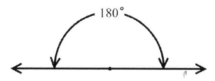

When two lines intersect, they form two sets of congruent *vertical angles*. The total measure of the angles is 360 degrees.

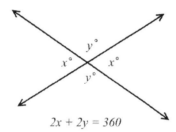

When two *parallel lines* are both intersected by a third line, they form two sets of *congruent* angles.

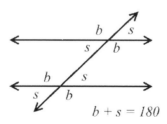

Circles

All *radii, r,* in a circle are equal.

The *diameter, d,* must go through the center of the circle. It is twice as long as the *radius* of the circle, and it is the longest line segment that can be contained in the circle.

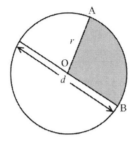

If a line segment doesn't pass through the center of a circle, it's just a chord.

The sum of the *central angles* in a circle is 360°.

Circumference, *C,* is the distance around a circle (think perimeter).

$$C = 2\pi r = \pi d$$

Area, *A,* is the amount of space occupied by a circle.

$$A = \pi r^2$$

Arc Length and *Sector Area* are related to the degree measure of the central angle.

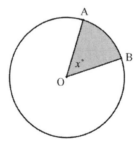

In the figure to the left, x is an example of a central angle.

$$\frac{x}{360} = \frac{m\widehat{AB}}{C_O} = \frac{aAOB}{A_O}$$

$m\widehat{AB}$: Length of arc $\widehat{AB}$
$aAOB$: Area of sector AOB
C_O: Circumference of Circle O
A_O: Area of Circle O

Triangles

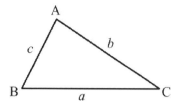

The sum of the interior angles in a triangle is 180 degrees.

$$\angle A + \angle B + \angle C = 180°$$

Third Side Rule

The length of any side of a triangle must be less than the sum of the lengths of the other two sides and greater than the difference of the lengths of the other two sides.

$$a - b < c < a + b$$

The bigger the opposite side, the bigger the angle, and vice versa.

If $A > B > C$, then $a > b > c$. And if $a > b > c$, then $A > B > C$.

$$A = \frac{1}{2}bh$$

Isosceles Triangles have at least two equal sides and two equal angles.

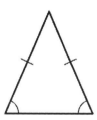

Equilateral Triangles have three equal sides and three 60° angles.

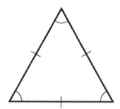

Right Triangles

Pythagorean Theorem: $a^2 + b^2 = c^2$

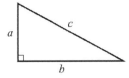

The two legs of a right triangle are also the base and height.

Special Right Triangles

45° - 45° - 90° Triangles are *isosceles* right triangles; the lengths of the sides always follow a $s : s : s\sqrt{2}$ ratio.

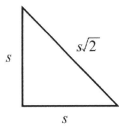

A square can be split into two 45°-45°-90° triangles.

isosceles: a triangle in which at least two sides (and thus two angles) are equal

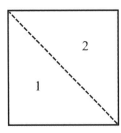

30° - 60° - 90° Triangles are *scalene* right triangles; the lengths of the sides always follow a $s : s\sqrt{3} : 2s$ ratio.

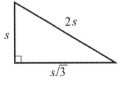

scalene: a triangle in which all three sides (and thus all three angles) are different

An equilateral triangle can be split into two 30° - 60° - 90° triangles.

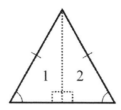

Similar Triangles

Triangles are *similar* if their angles are congruent. Corresponding sides are *proportional*.

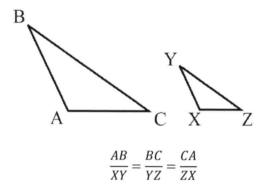

$$\frac{AB}{XY} = \frac{BC}{YZ} = \frac{CA}{ZX}$$

Common Geometry Triggers

If you see a...	you should...
weird shape,	use your pencil to create more familiar shapes.
equilateral triangle,	draw a 30 - 60 - 90 triangle.
diagonal of a square,	draw a 45 - 45 - 90 triangle.
set of overlapping shapes,	focus on shared sides/points/angles.
pair of parallel lines,	mark big and small angles.
blank space,	draw a figure.

Quadrilaterals

The sum of the interior angles is 360°.

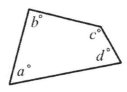

$$a + b + c + d = 360$$

Parallelograms

Opposite sides are parallel. Adjacent angles are supplementary (they add to 180°).

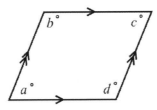

Common Mistake Alert
Unless the parallelogram is rectangular…
$a + c \neq 180$ and $b + d \neq 180$

$$a + b = 180 \quad b + c = 180 \quad c + d = 180 \quad d + a = 180$$

Squares

All angles are 90°. All sides are equal and opposite sides are parallel.

A square can be split into two 45°-45°-90° triangles. This is useful when dealing with the diagonal.

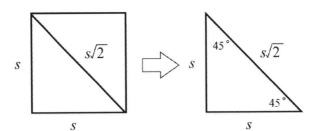

For squares…

$$A = s^2$$

$$P = 4s$$

Rectangles

All angles are 90°. Opposite sides are equal.

$A = lw$

$P = 2l + 2w$

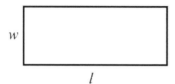

Trapezoids

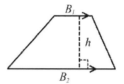

Trapezoids have two bases (B_1 and B_2), which are parallel.

$$A = \frac{B_1 + B_2}{2} \times h$$

Polygons

To find the sum of the measure of the interior angles of an n-sided polygon, use $Sum = (n - 2)180$

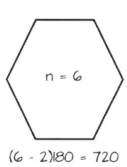

$(6 - 2)180 = 720$

Solid Geometry

Volume, V, is the three-dimensional space occupied by a solid shape.

Surface Area, SA, is the two-dimensional sum of the areas of the individual faces of a solid shape.

Cubes

Cubes have six faces. All six faces are squares with congruent edges.

$V = s^3$

$SA = 6s^2$

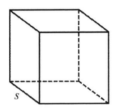

Rectangular Prisms

This solid shape is made of 3 pairs of congruent rectangles.

$V = lwh$

$SA = 2(lw + wh + lh)$

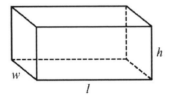

Spheres

Spheres are like three dimensional circles. The longest line you can draw in a sphere is its diameter.

$$V = \frac{4}{3}\pi r^3$$

$$SA = 4\pi r^2$$

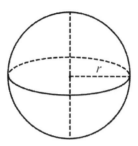

Cylinders

The top and bottom of a cylinder are circles.

$$V = \pi r^2 h$$

$$SA = 2\pi r^2 + 2\pi rh$$

Cones

The base of a cone is a circle.

$$V = \frac{1}{3}\pi r^2 h$$

Coordinate Geometry

Slope

$$Slope = m = \frac{rise}{run} = \frac{\Delta y}{\Delta x} = \frac{y_2 - y_1}{x_2 - x_1}$$

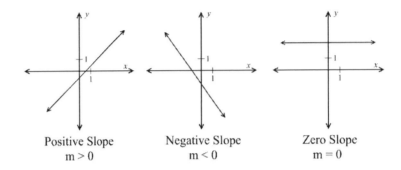

Positive Slope   Negative Slope   Zero Slope
m > 0   m < 0   m = 0

Linear Equations

Slope-Intercept Form: $y = mx + b$ where m is the slope and b is the y-intercept.
Point Slope Form: $m(x - x_1) = (y - y_1)$ where m is the slope and (x_1, y_2) is a point on the line.

Parallel lines have equal slopes.
Perpendicular lines have negative reciprocal slopes.

Distance

The distance formula is really just the Pythagorean Theorem in disguise.

$$c^2 = a^2 + b^2 \;\rightarrow\; c = \sqrt{a^2 + b^2}$$

$$D = \sqrt{(x_2 - x_1)^2 + (y_2 - y_1)^2}$$

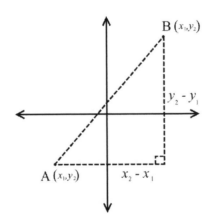

Distance in Three Dimensions

To find the distance between two points in three dimensions, use the Mega Pythagorean Theorem

$$a^2 + b^2 + c^2 = d^2$$

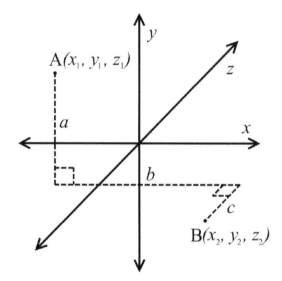

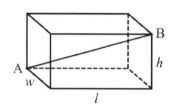

$$a = y_2 - y_1$$

$$b = x_2 - x_1$$

$$c = z_2 - z_1$$

$$AB = \sqrt{w^2 + l^2 + h^2}$$

You should know the signs of the coordinates in the different Quadrants:

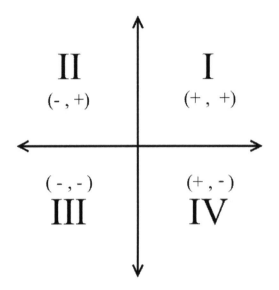

It's also helpful to be able to eyeball slopes:

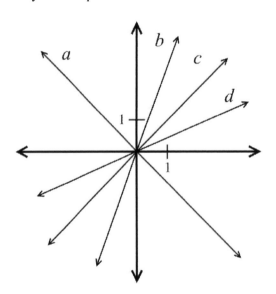

Can you estimate the slopes of the above lines?

a: _____   b: _____

c: _____   d: _____

a: -1, b: 2, c: 1, d: $\frac{1}{2}$

No Figure?

The SAT is remarkably good about providing figures with geometry questions. However, you shouldn't let that become a crutch, as there are generally three or four questions per test that require you to draw your own figure.

RTFQ: PLEASE READ THE FLIPPIN' QUESTION BEFORE YOU BEGIN DRAWING.

That is all.

The Geometry Approach

1. Get all information from the question on the figure.
   a. No figure? Draw one!
   b. Figure not drawn to scale? Redraw it or be VERY careful.
2. Info Dump
   a. What are relevant formulas?
   b. What are relevant facts?
3. Relate the provided info to the objective.
   a. Determine which formula is helpful.
   b. Determine which facts get you from the question to the answer.
4. If you're still not there, get creative! (optional)
   a. Estimate
   b. Use Your Own Numbers

16

Point B is a vertex of a 6-sided polygon. The polygon has 6 sides of equal length and 6 angles of equal measure. When all possible diagonals are drawn from point B to the other vertices in the polygon, how many non-overlapping triangles are formed?

24

The edges of a rectangular solid have lengths 3x, 4x, and 6x. What is the total surface area of the solid?

A) $72x$

B) $72x^2$

C) $108x^2$

D) $144x^2$

17

Five different points A, B, C, D, and E lie on a line in that order. The length of AD is 5.5 and the length of BE is 3.5. If the length of CD is 3, what is one possible value for the length of BC ?

31

Points R and S are on the surface of a sphere that has a volume of 288π cubic inches. What is the greatest possible length, in inches, of line segment $\overline{RS}$?

(The volume of a sphere with radius r is $V = \frac{4}{3}\pi r^3$.)

Getting Creative

The Geometry Approach

1. Get all information from the question on the figure.
    a. No figure? Draw one!
2. Info Dump
    a. What are relevant formulas?
    b. What are relevant facts?
3. Relate the provided information to the objective.
    a. Determine which formula is helpful.
    b. Determine which facts get you from the question to the answer.
4. If you're still not there, get creative!
    a. Estimate.
    b. Use Your Own Numbers.

Let's focus on step 4, shall we?

Figures on the SAT **are drawn to scale:**

1. Angles will be accurately drawn.
2. Dimensions will be consistent throughout the figure.
3. Similar shapes will have similar characteristics.

So let's say we have this figure and need to find the length of AB, but don't know how.

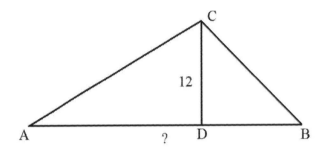

We may not know the length of AB, but we do know the length of CD. So let's make a ruler. Mark off the length of CD on the edge of your answer sheet…

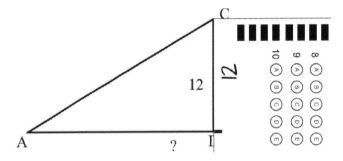

…and use that length to estimate the length of AB. Like so:

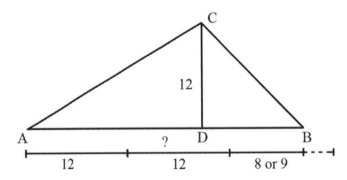

So by estimating, we can say with confidence that the length of AB is around 32 or 33. That should help us get rid of a few answer choices. Nice.

We can do the same thing with angles. Let's say we need to find the value of the following angle:

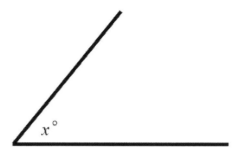

We can use the corner of our answer sheet to draw a perfect 90° reference angle…

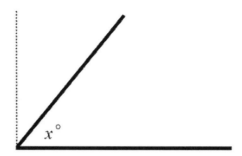

OK, that angle looks like it's a little more than half of the 90° angle you drew. 50° seems like a safe guess. Again, you can use this information to eliminate 2 - 4 of the answer choices.

Lastly, we can use shapes we're comfortable with to make estimates about shapes that are a little more troublesome. Let's take a look at a difficult question:

31

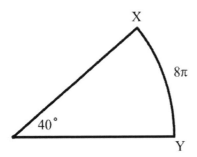

The figure above shows a portion of a circle whose central angle measures 40°. If the length of arc XY is 8π, what is the area of the figure?

A) 144π
B) 72π
C) 64π
D) 36π

Let's say we have done the first three steps of the Geometry approach, but still don't know how to find the answer. Let's try to estimate.

Well, that wedge shape is pretty similar to a triangle, which is way easier to work with:

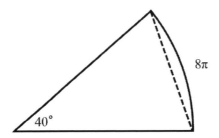

The length of the arc above is 8π, which is a little more than 25. The (dotted) line you just drew must be a little shorter than that. Let's say 24. Use the techniques described above to find the base and height of this "triangle."

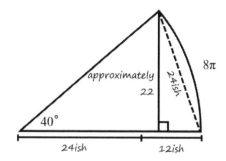

Using $A = \frac{1}{2}bh$, we can estimate the area of "triangle" to be around 396. Let's take a look at the answer choices:

A) $144\pi \approx 452$ pretty close
B) $72\pi \approx 226$ too small
C) $64\pi \approx 201$ too small
D) $36\pi \approx 113$ too small

How much do you want to bet that (A) is the correct answer?

Using Your Own Numbers

Just like with some algebra questions, sometimes it's easier to use your own numbers than to try to solve algebraically. Let's take a look at an example:

24

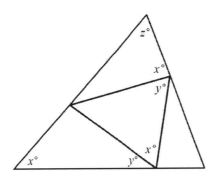

In the figure above, what is the value of z in terms of x and y?

A) $360 - 2x - 3y$
B) $180 - x - y$
C) $2x + 2y - 180$
D) $x + 3y - 180$

We see the phrase "in terms of," which tells us we have the option of using our own numbers.

Make up values for x and y and put them in the figure:

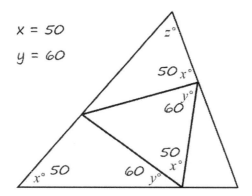

x = 50
y = 60

Use those values to find the missing angles, including z:

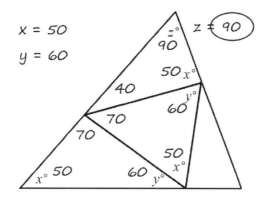

x = 50
y = 60

z = 90

We have our target. Let's find it in the answer choices:

A) $360 - 3x - 2y$ $360 - 3(50) - 2(60) = 90$ yep
B) $180 - x - y$ $180 - 50 - 60 = 70$ nope
C) $2x + 2y - 180$ $2(50) + 2(60) - 180 = 40$ nope
D) $3x + y - 180$ $3(50) + 60 - 180 = 30$ nope

180 Degrees in a Straight Line

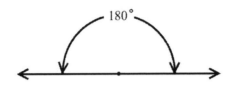

The title says it all. You have to look for it.

4

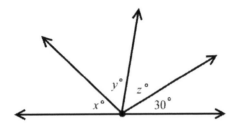

In the figure above, what is the value of $x + y + z$?

A) 130
B) 140
C) 150
D) 160

17

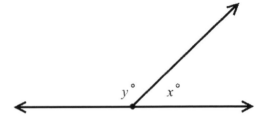

In the figure above, $y = 3x$. What is the value of y?

16

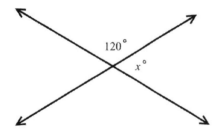

In the figure above, two lines intersect as shown.
What is the value of x?

180 Degrees in a Triangle

All the angles in a triangle have to add up to 180°. This is a *fundamental* truth. This single concept will earn you at least ten points on the SAT.

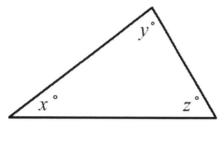

$$x + y + z = 180$$

In a right triangle, the two non-right angles always add up to 90°.

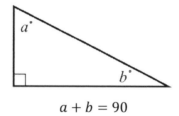

$$a + b = 90$$

Thinking about it this way will make things easier.

fundamental: adj, serving as, or being an essential part of, a foundation or basis; basic; underlying

2

17

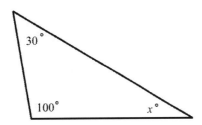

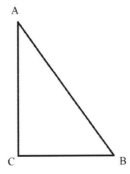

In the figure above, what is the value of *x* ?

A) 30
B) 40
C) 50
D) 60

In triangle ABC, the measure of angle A is half the measure of angle B, and the measure of angle C is three times the measure of angle A. What is the degree measure of angle A ?

Bonus: Finding the Sum of Interior Angles

You can use this concept to find the total number of degrees in any polygon you'll see on the SAT. Just pick a vertex and draw lines to all the other vertices to create triangles.

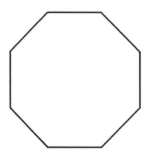 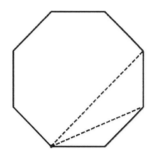 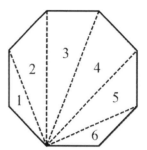

$$6\ Triangles \times 180° = 1080°$$

35

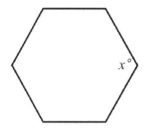

The figure above is a regular hexagon. What is the degree measure of the angle marked x ?

A) 100
B) 120
C) 150
D) 160

Or you can memorize this formula…

⊕ ⊖   **Sum of Interior Angles of an n-sided Polygon**

⊘ ⊗ $(n - 2)180° = sum\ of\ interior\ angles$

Circles

Most circle questions boil down to finding the radius and then doing something with it. Every circle formula uses the radius. Let's review.

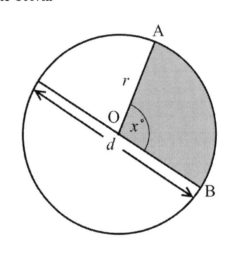

Circle Trivia

Diameter: $D = 2r$

Circumference: $C = 2\pi r \text{ or } \pi d$

Area: $A = \pi r^2$

Arc Length: $\dfrac{x°}{360°} = \dfrac{\widehat{mAB}}{2\pi r}$

Sector Area: $\dfrac{x°}{360°} = \dfrac{areaAOB}{\pi r^2}$

Important Facts
There are $360°$ in a circle.
All radii are equal.

16

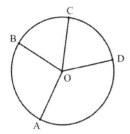

Points A, B, C, and D lie on a circle with center O. If the radius of the circle is 2, what is the value of $AO + BO + CO + DO$?

9

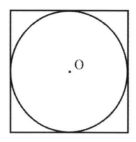

In the figure above, a circle with center O is inscribed in a square of area 64 square inches. What is the circumference of the circle, in inches?

A) 8π

B) 16π

C) 32π

D) 64π

8

Circles A and B have radii of 2 and 3, respectively. How much greater is the circumference of circle B than the circumference of circle A ?

A) $\frac{2\pi}{3}$

B) π

C) $\frac{3\pi}{2}$

D) 2π

33

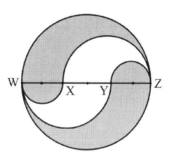

Semicircular arcs WX, XY, XZ, and YZ divide the circle above into regions. The points shown along the diameter WZ divide it into 6 equal parts. If WZ = 12, what is the total perimeter of the unshaded region?

A) 4π

B) 6π

C) 12π

D) 24π

One last note: π isn't as scary as it looks. Treat it like a variable.

360 Degrees in a Circle

The sum of the angles formed in the center of a circle is always 360°.

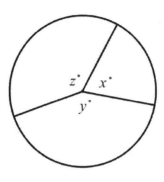

$$x + y + z = 360$$

This is true even when there's no circle.

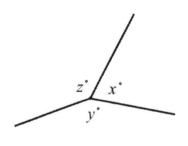

$$x + y + z = 360$$

Try applying this concept to a few SAT questions.

6

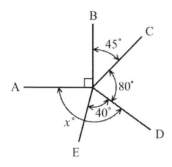

In the figure above, what is the value of x ?

A) 105
B) 125
C) 145
D) 165

7

Points C and D lie on a circle whose center is O. If the length of arc $\overarc{CD}$ is $\frac{1}{12}$ of the circumference of the circle, what is the measure of $\angle COD$?

A) 20
B) 30
C) 40
D) 50

Trigonometry

Right-triangle trigonometry is all about **SOHCAHTOA.**

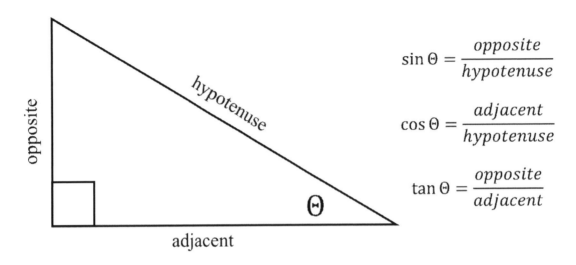

$$\sin \Theta = \frac{opposite}{hypotenuse}$$

$$\cos \Theta = \frac{adjacent}{hypotenuse}$$

$$\tan \Theta = \frac{opposite}{adjacent}$$

Remember:

1. The designations OPPOSITE and ADJACENT are relative to the angle of interest (in this case, theta). The HYPOTENUSE is never either of these.
2. There's a big difference between $\sin \theta$ and $\sin^{-1} \theta$.
   a. If the question provides you with the angle and asks for the side length, use sin, cos, or tan in your calculator.
   b. If the question provides you with the sides and asks for the angle measure, use $\sin^{-1}$, $\cos^{-1}$, or $\tan^{-1}$ in your calculator.
3. You WILL get the wrong answer if your calculator is in the wrong mode.
   a. If the angle measure is in radians (there will usually be a π somewhere), use RADIAN mode.
   b. If the angle measure is in degrees (look for a ° sign), use DEGREE mode.

18

In a right triangle, one angle is θ radians and $\cos \theta = \frac{3}{5}$. What is $\sin(\frac{\pi}{2} - \theta)$?

20

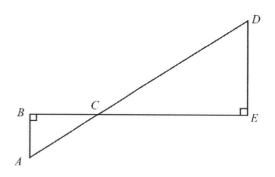

In the figure above, $AB = 6$, $AC = 10$, and $DE = 15$. What is the value of $\cos D$?

19

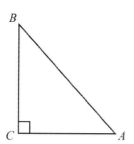

In right triangle ABC above, the sine of angle A is 0.8. What is the tangent of angle B ?

24

Two acute angles, x and y, exist such that $\sin(x°) = \cos(y°)$. If $x + y = \frac{n}{3}$, what is the value of n ?

Fun fact: for any two angles a and b such $a + b = 90$, $\sin a = \cos b$ (or $\cos b = \sin a$.

Functions and Graphs Introduction

A function can be thought of as a machine that transforms an input into an output.

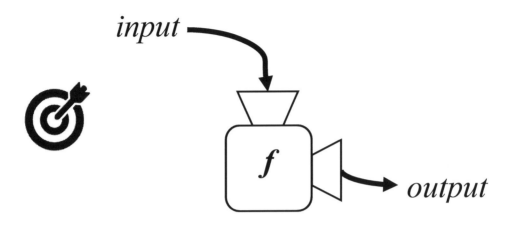

The Input, Function, and Output can appear in several different forms:

Input	Function	Output
Independent Variable	Equation, Word Description or Graph	Dependent Variable
x	Equation (e.g., $y = 2x + 6$)	$f(x)$ or y
a, b, n, etc...	Letter Designation (e.g., $f, g, P, function\ name$)	$f(a), g(b), P(n),$ $function\ name(etc)$
Horizontal axis	Graph in xy-coordinate plane	Vertical axis

Additionally, there are really only three different varieties of Functions & Graphs questions on the SAT. Each type will require a slightly different approach.

TYPE I

The question provides the function and input, but not the output.

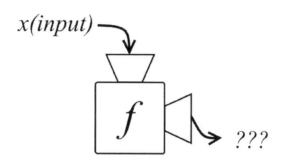

TYPE II

The question provides the function and output, but not the input.

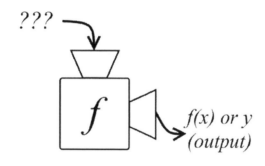

TYPE III

The question provides the input and output, but not the function.

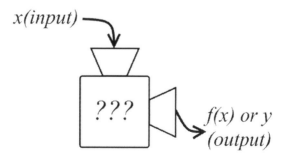

That's it. Getting good at Function & Graphs questions is simply a matter of figuring out which scenario you're dealing with and taking the appropriate course of action. The next set of modules will walk you through each of these categories.

Building and Interpreting Linear Functions

Linear relationships are generally expressed in *slope-intercept form:*

$$y = mx + b$$

You'd seen it a million times, sure. But there's useful information in there. For instance…

…if you wanted to model the price of a pizza as a function of number of toppings,

Big Italy Pizzeria

Large Cheese Pizza …… $15
Toppings……………… $1.50/topping

In the function $y = mx + b$:

- ✓ *y*: final price of the pizza
- ✓ *x*: number of toppings
- ✓ *m*: price per topping
- ✓ *b*: starting price (plain pizza)

And…

- ✓ The *y*-intercept of that line would be the price of a large cheese pizza with no other toppings and
- ✓ The slope of the line would be the price per topping.

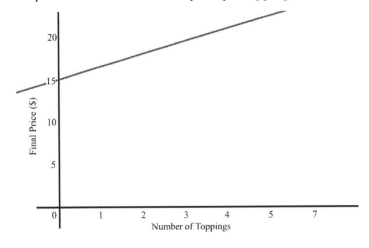

Or if want to model the model the cost of a cell phone plan that charges a flat $20 per month and $0.10 per minute, your function would be:

$$c(m) = 0.10m + 20$$

Where:

✓ c: the cost of the monthly bill
✓ m: the number of minutes used

What would the graph that function look like? (Don't forget to label the axes.)

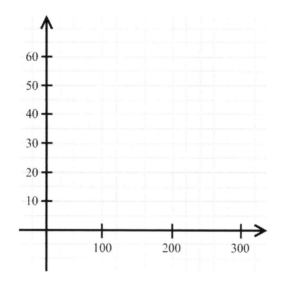

Hint:

You may need to do some unit conversion before graphing.

What Does the Slope of a Linear Function Represent?

Since slope $= \dfrac{\Delta y}{\Delta x}$, place the vertical axis unit in the numerator and the horizontal axis unit in the denominator to determine what the ratio represents.

Examples:

$\dfrac{\Delta\,miles}{\Delta\,hours}$ represents miles per hour

$\dfrac{\Delta\,population}{\Delta\,years}$ represents population growth per year

$\dfrac{\Delta\,total\,cost}{\Delta\,units}$ represents change in total cost per unit produced

7

The monthly sales for Yusuf's World of Falafel from January to December 2010 can be modeled by the equation $y = 2,600x + 27,200$, where x represents the number of months since the beginning of the year, and y represents the monthly sales amount. Which of the following best describes the meaning of the number 2,600 in the equation?

A) The total sales in January of 2010
B) The total sales per month in 2010
C) The increase in the monthly sales amount in 2010
D) The difference between the monthly sales in January and the monthly sales in December

12

A high school theater production of *Our Town* sells 270 tickets for a Friday night performance. Adult tickets cost 6 dollars each and children's tickets cost 4 dollar each. If the school raises $1,280 from Friday night's ticket sales, which of the following systems of equations can be used to find the number of children and adult tickets sold?

A) $a + c = 1280$
$6a + 4c = 270$
B) $6a + 4c = 1280$
$a + c = 270$
C) $6a + 4c = 1280$
$a + c = 270$
D) $a + 4c = 1280$
$6a + c = 270$

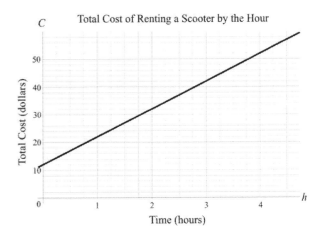

The graph above displays the total cost C, in dollars, of renting a scooter for h hours.

16

What does the C-intercept represent in the graph?

A) The total number of hours that the scooter is rented
B) The total number of scooters rented
C) The initial cost of renting the scooter
D) The increase I cost to rent the scooter for each additional hour

17

If the relationship between h and C can be modeled with the equation $C(h) = 10h + 11$, what does the number 10 represent?

A) The flat rate charged to rent the scooter before any hours are accrued
B) The hourly rate of renting the scooter
C) The average total cost for renting a scooter over an h-hour period
D) The total number of hours for which the scooter is rented

Type I – Input and Function are Provided

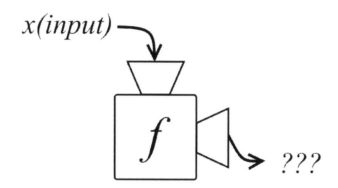

Remember: $f(x) = x^2 + 4x + 5$ is the same EXACT function as $y = x^2 + 4x + 5$.

Questions that provide the input are generally the easiest function questions because they're most similar to what you do in school: Put whatever is in the parentheses into the function:

If $f(x) = x^3 + 5x$, then $f(4) = 4^3 + 5(4)$
and
$f(n + 5) = (n + 5)^3 + 5(n + 5)$

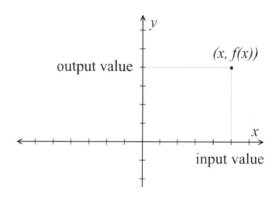

Type I Functions

- If you have a traditional $f(x)$ equation…
  - replace the variable inside the parentheses with the new input, and
  - calculate the value of the function with that new input.
- If you have the graph of a function…
  - draw a vertical line at the provided input and find where it hits the graph
  - The vertical value of the graph is your answer.
- If you have a list of inputs and outputs…
  - find the output that corresponds with the indicated input.

5

If $f(x) = 5x^2 + 3x - 4$, what is the value of
$f(5) - f(2)$?

A) 3
B) 74
C) 101
D) 114

16

$$P(n) = 2,000 \times 2^{\frac{n}{4}}$$

Some bacteria are being cultured in a Petri dish.
The population, P, of the bacteria in the dish n days
after the culture began is modeled by the function
above. By how many bacteria does the population
increase from $n = 8$ to $n = 12$?

30

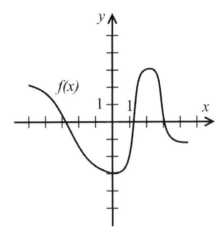

The figure above shows the graph of the function f.
Which of the following is greater than $f(-4)$?

A) $f(-1)$
B) $f(2)$
C) $f(3)$
D) $f(4)$

17

The estimated resale value, in dollars, of a car is
given by the function $r(t) = ct + 12,000$, where
the integer t is the number of years after the car
was purchased, $0 \le t \le 10$, and c is a constant.
The estimated resale value of the car 5 years after
the purchase is $6,000. What is the estimated
value, in dollars, of the car 9 years after the
purchase?
(Disregard the $ sign when gridding your answer.)

Type II – Function and Output are Provided

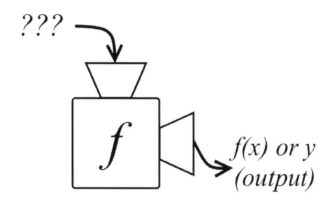

When the question gives you the function and the output, the test is simply asking you what you would have to put *into* the function to get a specific output. For many of these questions, you can simply set the function equal to the output and solve for the input.

Type II Functions

- If you have a traditional $f(x)$ equation...
    - set the functions equal to the provided output, and
    - solve for the unknown input variable.
- If you have the graph of a function...
    - draw a horizontal line at the provided output and find where it hits the graph.
    - The horizontal value of the graph is your answer. (note: you may have more than one point of intersection)
- If you have a list of inputs and outputs...
    - find the input that corresponds with the indicated output.

16

The function f is defined as $f(x) = x^2 + 4$. If t is a positive integer and $f(t) = 20$, what is the value of t ?

17

In dry air, the speed of a cannonball V, in meters per second, is modeled by the function $V(t) = 331.4 + 0.6t$, where t is the temperature in degrees Celsius. According to the model, for what value of t is the speed of a cannonball in dry air 343.7 meters per second?

19

$$f(x) = |3x - 19|$$

For the function defined above, what is one possible value of b for which $f(b) < b$?

32

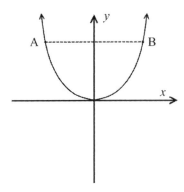

In the figure above, the parabola is the graph of $y = x^2$. If the y-coordinate of A and the y-coordinate of B are each 8, what is the length of AB ?

A) 16
B) 8
C) $4\sqrt{2}$
D) $2\sqrt{2}$

18

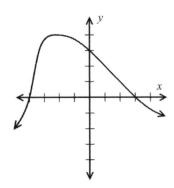

The graph above shows the graph of f. If $r > s$, $f(r) = 0$, and $f(s) = 0$, what is the value of r^s ?

Type III – Input and Output are Provided

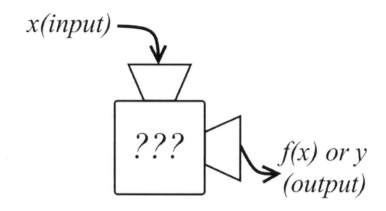

Once in a while, a question will describe a function or provide you with a set of inputs and outputs. You can usually get the answer by testing out the function with the information the question provides or making up your own input or output.

Remember: if you're provided multiple inputs and outputs, *all numbers must work with the correct function.*

Type III Functions

- If you have a traditional $f(x)$ equation...
  - replace the variable inside the parentheses with the provided input,
  - set the function equal to the provided output,
  - and find the value of the unknown values in the function.
- If you have the graph of a function...
  - use characteristics such as slope, y-intercept, and transformations to identify the correct graph or equation.
- If you have a list of inputs and outputs...
  - test all of the input and output values.
  - Select the function that produces true statements with *all* of the inputs and outputs.

18

x	2	3	4	5
$f(x)$	7	12	19	28

The table above shows certain values of the function f. Which of the following could be $f(x)$?

A) $f(x) = 2x + 3$
B) $f(x) = x^3 - 1$
C) $f(x) = 4x + 3$
D) $f(x) = x^2 + 3$

9

At Wise Guys Pizza Parlor, it costs $18.00 for a plain cheese pizza, plus $1.50 for each topping. If the function $P(t)$ represents the price, in dollars, of a cheese pizza with t toppings, which of the following is true?

A) $P(t) = 18.00 + 1.50$
B) $P(t) = 18.00 + 1.50t$
C) $P(t) = 18.00t + 1.50$
D) $t = 18.00 + 1.50P(t)$

30

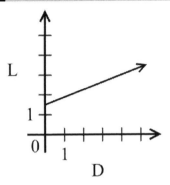

A science student graphed the length of a tadpole over time, and the results are shown above. If L represents the length of the tadpole in millimeters and D represents the number of the day from when he started measuring, which of the following equations best describes the data shown?

A) $L = 3D + 1.5$
B) $L = 3D - 1.5$
C) $L = \frac{1}{3}D + 1.5$
D) $L = 4.5D + 1.5$

36

x	$f(x)$
0	4
1	5
2	12
3	31
4	68
5	129
6	220

Several values of $f(x)$ are shown above. If $g(x) = f(2x + 2)$, what is the value of $g(1)$?

A) 5
B) 31
C) 68
D) 129

17

Let f be a function such that $f(x) = |x| - c$, where c is a constant. If $f(-5) = -2$, what is the value of $f(-7)$?

19

In the xy-plane, the line $4x - 2y = d$ passes through point $(6, -1)$. What is the value of d ?

32

x	$f(x)$
1	4
2	6
3	8
4	10
5	12
6	14
7	16

Several values of the function f are shown above. The function g is defined by $g(x) = f(2x + 3)$. What is the value of $g(2)$?

24

p	$f(p)$
2	3
4	5
6	7
8	9
10	11

The function f is defined by the table above. For what value of p does $f(p) = 2p - 7$?

A) 2
B) 4
C) 6
D) 8

Quadratic Functions

Problems involving quadratic functions test your ability to recognize the three most common quadratic functions:

$$(x + y)^2 = x^2 + 2xy + y^2$$
$$(x - y)^2 = x^2 - 2xy + y^2$$
$$(x + y)(x - y) = x^2 - y^2$$

You need to have these memorized. Luckily, if you remember the left-hand side of each equation, you can generate the right-hand side by *FOILing*.

If you know those three equations, most questions can be solved by recognizing which one is relevant and determining the value of the missing pieces. There is usually no other way to solve these types of questions. You just have to know the equations.

Give it a try.

16.

If $(a + b)^2 = 64$ and $(a - b)^2 = 16$, what is the value of ab ?

A) 6
B) 12
C) 24
D) 48

32

If $x^2 + y^2 = 16$, and $(x - y)^2 = 10$, what is the value of xy ?

A) 2
B) 3
C) 4
D) 6

FOIL stands for First, Outer, Inner, Last. Use this technique to multiply two binomials.

Example
$$(a + b)(c - d) = ac - ad + bc - bd$$

18

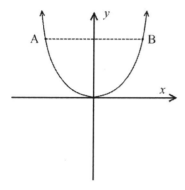

In the figure above, the parabola is the graph of $y = \frac{1}{2}x^2$. If the y-coordinate of A and the y-coordinate of B are each 8, what is the length of $\overline{AB}$?

A) 4
B) 8
C) 12
D) 16

32

For all a in the domain of the function $\frac{a+1}{a^3-a}$, this function equivalent to:

A) $\frac{1}{a^2} - \frac{1}{a^3}$

B) $\frac{1}{a^3} - \frac{1}{a}$

C) $\frac{1}{a^2-1}$

D) $\frac{1}{a^2-a}$

Don't forget: parabolas and are symmetrical.

131

Useful Quadratic Forms

Standard Form

$$ax^2 + bx + c = f(x)$$

Where axis of symmetry is $x = -\dfrac{b}{2a}$

If $a > 0$, the parabola opens up, and if $a < 0$, the parabola opens down.

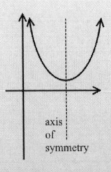

axis
of
symmetry

Vertex Form

$$a(x - h)^2 + k = f(x)$$

Where axis of symmetry is $x = h$ and the vertex is at (h, k).

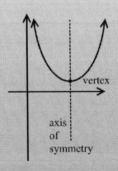

vertex

axis
of
symmetry

Putting an equation into this form may require you to use the "completing the square" method.

29

$$f(x) = (x - 5)(x + 3)$$

Which of the following is an equivalent form of the function f above in which the minimum value of f appears as a constant or coefficient?

A) $f(x) = x^2 - 15$
B) $f(x) = x^2 + 2x - 15$
C) $f(x) = (x - 1)^2 - 16$
D) $f(x) = (x - 1)^2 - 14$

13

$$y = g(x - 3)(x + 5)$$

In the equation above, g is a nonzero constant. The graph of the equation in the xy-plane is a parabola with vertex (h, k). Which of the following is equal to k?

A) $-16g$
B) $-12g$
C) $-6g$
D) $-2g$

Finding Solutions of Quadratics

When a quadratic is set equal to zero, some interesting characteristics start to emerge. We can find zeroes/roots/solutions using two key methods.

$$ax^2 + bx + c = 0$$

Factoring

$$(dx + p)(gx + q) = 0$$

Where $dg = a$, $pq = c$, and $dg + pq = b$

The Quadratic Formula

$$x = \frac{-b \pm \sqrt{b^2 - 4ac}}{2a}$$

Note: make sure your quadratic is set equal to ZERO *before* attempting either of these methods.

12

What are the solutions to $x^2 + 10x + 7 = 2$?

A) $x = -5 \pm 2\sqrt{5}$

B) $x = -5 \pm \frac{\sqrt{5}}{2}$

C) $x = -10 \pm 2\sqrt{5}$

D) $x = -10 + \sqrt{5}$

14

$$x^2 - \frac{b}{2}x = 2q$$

In the quadratic equation above, b and q are constants. What are the solutions for x ?

A) $x = \frac{b}{4} \pm \frac{\sqrt{b^2 + 2q}}{4}$

B) $x = \frac{b}{4} \pm \frac{\sqrt{b^2 + 32q}}{4}$

C) $x = \frac{b}{2} \pm \frac{\sqrt{b^2 + 2q}}{2}$

D) $x = \frac{b}{2} \pm \frac{\sqrt{b^2 + 32q}}{4}$

Transformations

There are handful of transformations that can change the size and location of the graph of a function. Let's review, going from least to most complex.

Vertical and Horizontal Translations

Here's a basic function, $y = x^2$ Here's $y = x^2 + 2$

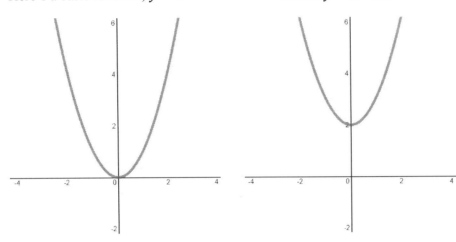

See the difference? Same graph; just shifted up two units.

Here's $y = x^2$ again.   Now here's $y = (x + 2)^2$

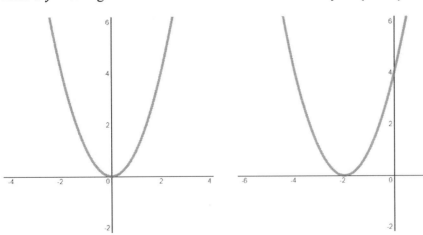

This time, the graph moves horizontally. However, the translation is reversed. Adding 2 inside the parentheses moves the graph two units to the *left*.

Translations don't change the shape of a graph. They only move them around.

Reflections

Here is $y = x^2 + 2$.

And here's $y = -(x^2 + 2)$

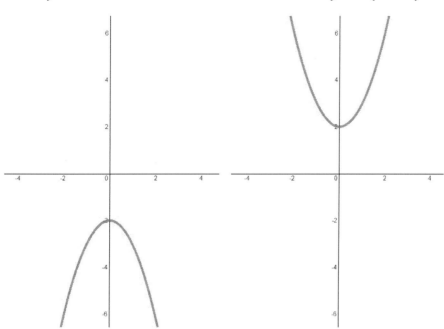

Flipping the sign of the *entire* function will reflect the graph across the *x*-axis.

Here's $y = (x + 2)^2$.

And here's $y = (-x + 2)^2$

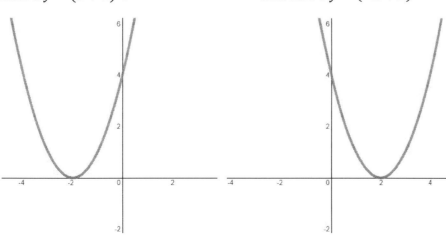

Changing the sign of the *x* term will flip the graph across the *y*-axis.

Stretches and Squeezes

Here's $y = x^2$ $\qquad\qquad\qquad$ $y = 2(x^2)$ $\qquad\qquad\qquad$ $y = \frac{1}{2}(x^2)$

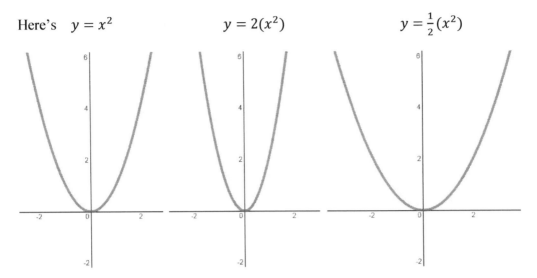

Adding a multiplier on the outside of the function will change the *steepness* of the graph. The bigger the absolute value of the multiplier, the steeper the graph.

Compare $y = x^2$ $\qquad\qquad$ $y = (2x)^2$ $\qquad\qquad\qquad$ $y = (\frac{1}{2}x)^2$

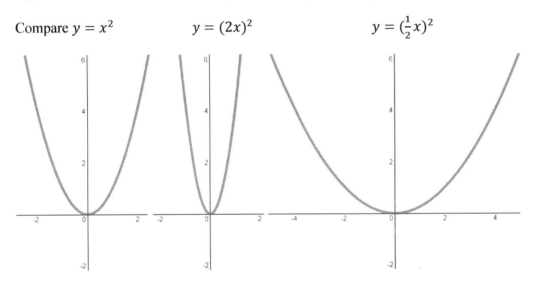

Adding a multiplier on the inside of the function will change the *width* of the graph. Bigger values will make the graph narrower and smaller ones will make the graph wider.

Weird Transformations

You already know that the absolute value operator makes negative numbers positive. It does the same thing to graphs of functions.

Here's $y = x^2 - 4$.   Check out $y = |x^2 - 4|$

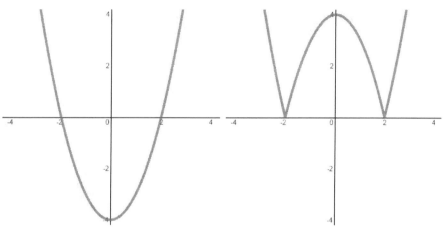

Slapping a pair of absolute value signs around a function will transform the graph in a very particular way. Since absolute value only changes the value of negative numbers, it also will only reflect the portions of the graph that are under the x-axis (the negative outputs).

11

Which of the following equations has a graph in the xy-plane for which y is always greater than or equal to -2 ?

A) $y = |x| - 3$
B) $y = x^2 - 3$
C) $y = (x - 3)^2$
D) $y = x^3 - 3$

26

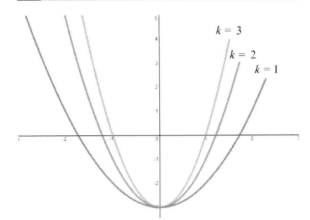

The three parabolas graphed in the standard (x, y) coordinate plane above are from a family of parabolas. A general equation that defines the family of parabolas contains the variable k in addition to x and y. For one of the parabolas shown, $k = 1$; for another, $k = 2$; and for the third, $k = 3$. Which of the following could be the general equation that defines this family of parabolas for all positive values of k ?

A) $y = kx^2 - 3$
B) $y = \frac{1}{k}x^2 - 3$
C) $y = -kx^2 - 3$
D) $y = -\frac{1}{k}x^2 - 3$

17

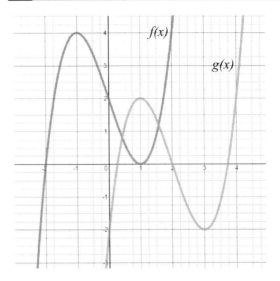

The graph above contains the functions $f(x)$ and $g(x)$. If $g(x) = f(x + h) - k$, what is the value of $h - k$?

A) -4
B) 0
C) 2
D) 4

Polynomials

The general form of a polynomial to the nth power is…

$$f(x) = a_n x^n + a_{n-1} x^{n-1} \ldots a_2 x^2 + a_1 x^1 + a_0$$

In addition to the skills covered in the Quadratics and Functions modules, the SAT will test you on four distinct skills related to polynomials. Let's review, going from least to most complicated.

Combining Like Terms

Quick Review

Rule	Example
If you're adding or subtracting terms that contain the same variable raised to the same power, just add or subject the coefficients.	$x^2 + 2x^2 = 3x^2$ $6n^4 - 9n^4 = -3n^4$ $5c^3 + 6c^3 = 5c^3 + 6c^3$
If you're multiplying terms with the same variables, *multiply* the coefficients and *add* the exponents.	$6a^2 \times 2a^5 = 12a^7$ $5x^4(3x^2 + 5x^3) = 15x^6 + 25x^7$
If you're dividing terms with the same variables, *divide* the coefficients and *subtract* the exponents.	$\dfrac{15x^{10}}{5x^8} = 3x^2$ $15x^5y^3 + 10x^2y = 5x^2y(3x^3y^2 + 2)$

3

Which of the following is equivalent to the sum of the expressions $x^2 - 1$ and $x^2 + 1$?

A) $x^2 + x$
B) $x^3 - 1$
C) $2x^2$
D) x^3

14

Which of the following is equivalent to $\left(x + \dfrac{y}{2}\right)^2$?

A) $x^2 + \dfrac{y^2}{2}$

B) $x^2 + \dfrac{x^2}{4}$

C) $x^2 + \dfrac{xy}{2} + \dfrac{y^2}{2}$

D) $x^2 + xy + \dfrac{y^2}{4}$

Finding Roots/Solutions/Zeroes/*x*-intercepts

You can know that $x + y = 0$ and not really know *anything* for sure about either x or y. There are lots of numbers that add up to zero.

However, if you know that $xy = 0$, can you say with *absolute certainty* that either x or y (or both) is equal to zero.

That's pretty cool.

Similarly, if you know that $x^2 + x = 42$, you can maybe intuitively see that there are two numbers that would create a true statement, but it'd be hard to say quickly what they are.

However, if you moved the 42 over to the other side of the equation…

$$x^2 + x - 42 = 0$$

…then factored the polynomial on the right…

$$(x + 7)(x - 6) = 0$$

…we now know that $x + 7 = 0$ or $x - 6 = 0$. That's pretty cool.

And that's all finding *x*-intercepts/roots/solutions/zeroes means. If you looking at the graph of $y = x^2 + x - 42$, you'll see that the graph crosses the *x*-axis at $x = -7$ and $x = 6$.

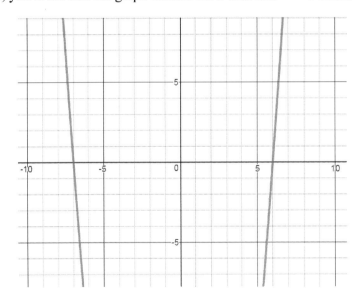

That's because $y = 0$ everywhere on the *x*-axis. See why that "the product of two numbers is equal to zero" thing is so useful?

5

Which of the following functions in the *xy*-plane has no *x*-intercepts?

A) A linear function with a non-zero rate of change
B) A cubic polynomial with at least one real zero
C) A quadratic function with real zeros
D) A quadratic function with no real zeros

10

$$y = x^2$$
$$y + 2 = -4x + 7$$

If *x* is a solution of the system of equations above, which of the following represents all real values of *x* ?

A) $\{-4, 1\}$
B) $\{-1, 4\}$
C) $\{-4, -1\}$
D) $\{1, 4\}$

19

What is the sum of the solutions to
$(x - 5)(x + .4) = 0$

A) -5.4
B) -4.6
C) 4.6
D) 5.4

18

$$x^3 - 4x^2 + 3x - 12 = 0$$

For what real value of *x* is the equation above true?

141

Finding Messy Factors

So we can all agree that factoring is great. But what if you're dealing with a polynomial that doesn't want to be factored?

$$y = 2x^2 + 12x - 3$$

You'll drive yourself crazy trying to factor that ish. Enter the **Quadratic Equation**.

For $y = ax^2 + bx + c$,

$$x = \frac{-b \pm \sqrt{b^2 - 4ac}}{2a}$$

The nice thing about the Quadratic Equation is that it works on any polynomial, *even if the polynomial is factorable.*

13

What are the solutions to $-2x^2 + 12x + 4 = 0$?

A) $x = 3 \pm \sqrt{10}$

B) $x = 3 \pm \frac{\sqrt{40}}{4}$

C) $x = -12 \pm \sqrt{10}$

D) $x = -12 + 4\sqrt{10}$

14

$$f(x) = 3x^2 - 8x - 7$$

What is the sum of the solutions to equation above?

A) $\frac{8}{3}$

B) $8 + \sqrt{37}$

C) 16

D) $\frac{74}{6}$

Slope-Intercept Form

Linear functions are easier to work with when they're in slope-intercept form.

Slope-Intercept Form of a Linear Function

$$y = mx + b$$

m: slope of the function
b: y-axis intercept

Since this form makes things easier, the first thing you're going to do when you see a linear function is **put it in slope-intercept form**.

Parallel lines have equal slopes.
Perpendicular lines have negative (or, *opposite*) reciprocal slopes.
The product of the slopes of two perpendicular lines is always -1.

16

In the xy-plane, line l is the graph of $2x + cy = 3$, where c is a constant. The graph of $4x + 10y = 5$ is parallel to line l. What is the value of c?

17

In the xy-plane, line l is the graph of $4x + cy = 6$ where c is a constant. The graph of $-4x + 20y = -10$ is perpendicular to line l. What is the value of c?

6

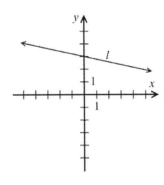

In the xy-plane above, the equation of line l is $x + 4y = 12$. Which of the following is an equation of a line that is perpendicular to line l?

A) $2x + 4y = 3$
B) $4x + y = 12$
C) $y = -4x + 2$
D) $\frac{1}{4}x + y = 3$

Slope

Slope is defined as

$$m = \frac{y_2 - y_1}{x_2 - x_1} = \frac{rise}{run}$$

It can also be thought of as the steepness of a function. Use the definition that helps you solve a problem.

But first, it's always good to be able to estimate.

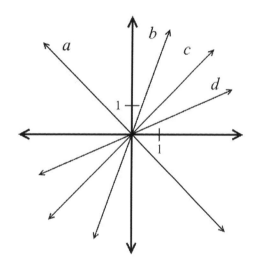

What are the approximate slopes of the following lines?

a: _____   b: _____

c: _____   d: _____

How can you quickly identify positive, negative, and zero slopes?

8

21

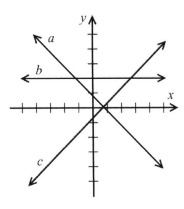

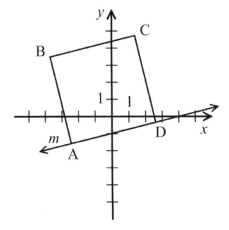

In the xy-coordinate plane above, the slopes of lines a, b, and c are x, y, and z, respectively. Which of the following gives the correct relationship of x, y, and z ?

A) $y < x < z$
B) $y < z < x$
C) $z < y < x$
D) $x < y < z$

In the xy-coordinate plane above, points A and D lie on line m as shown. If $ABCD$ is a square, what is the product of the slopes of line segments $\overline{AB}$ and $\overline{CD}$?

A) -16
B) $-\frac{1}{4}$
C) $\frac{1}{4}$
D) 16

Remember: Perpendicular lines have negative reciprocal slopes.

Coordinate Geometry and Conics

Many Coordinate Geometry questions are *subterfuge*; they're really just geometry questions with an additional feature. Sometime the addition of the *xy*-coordinate plane makes simple concepts a notch more complicated. The key to these questions is to either use something you know about coordinate plane to make a conclusion about the shape or use something you know about the shape to make a conclusion about the coordinate plane. It's always one or the other.

11

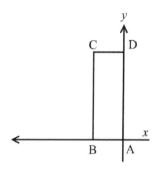

In the *xy*-plane above, the length of AD is 4 times the length of AB. If the *x*-coordinate of point B is −2, what is the area of rectangle ABCD ?

A) 4
B) 8
C) 16
D) 32

12

In the *xy*-coordinate plane, what is the area of the square with opposite vertices at (-3, -3) and (3, 3) ?

A) 18
B) 24
C) 27
D) 36

23

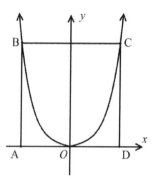

In the figure above, ABCD is a square and points B, C, and O lie on the graph of $y = 2cx^2$, where c is a constant. If the area of the square is 100, what is the value of c?

A) 0.2
B) 0.5
C) 1.0
D) 5

147

You'll also occasionally need to know formulas for circles, ellipses, and hyperbolas:

Equation of a Circle

$$(x - h)^2 + (y - k)^2 = r^2$$

Where the center of the circle is (h, k) and the radius is .

Equation of an Ellipse

$$\frac{x^2}{a^2} + \frac{y^2}{b^2} = 1 \qquad \text{or} \qquad \frac{(x-m)^2}{a^2} + \frac{(y-n)^2}{b^2} = 1$$

…when the ellipse is centered at the origin   …when the ellipse has a center at (m, n)

Right most point: $(m + a, n)$
Left most point: $(m - a, n)$
Top most point: $(m, n + b)$
Bottom most point: $(m, n - b)$

Equation of a Hyperbola

$$\frac{(x - m)^2}{a^2} - \frac{(y - n)^2}{b^2} = 1$$

These types of questions appear relatively infrequently.

Coordinate Geometry

- ✓ Don't confuse your x's and y's.
- ✓ Use the origin or axes.
  - o On the x-axis, the y value is always zero.
  - o On the y-axis, the x value is always zero.
  - o At the origin, x and y are both zero.
- ✓ Use rules of symmetry.
- ✓ If there's no figure, draw one!

22

An equation of a particular circle is
$(x - 4)^2 + y^2 = 6$. What are the coordinates of
this circle's center and what is the length, in
coordinate units, of this circle's radius?

	Center	**Radius**
A)	$(-4, 0)$	$\sqrt{6}$
B)	$(-4, 0)$	3
C)	$(4, 0)$	$\sqrt{6}$
D)	$(4, 0)$	6

23

$$x^2 + y^2 + 6x - 4y = 3$$

The equation of a circle in the xy-plane is show
above. What is the radius of the circle?

A) 2

B) 3

C) 4

D) 5

28

One of the following equations determines the
graph in the standard (x, y) coordinate plane
below. Which one?

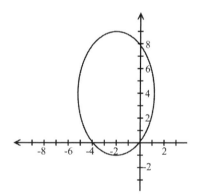

A) $\dfrac{(x-2)^2}{25} + \dfrac{(y-4)^2}{9} = 1$

B) $\dfrac{(x-2)^2}{25} + \dfrac{(y+4)^2}{9} = 1$

C) $\dfrac{(x+2)^2}{9} + \dfrac{(y-4)^2}{25} = 1$

D) $\dfrac{(x+2)^2}{9} + \dfrac{(y+4)^2}{25} = 1$

Average (Arithmetic Mean)

Ah, the *lowly* average. Take a few numbers, add them up, divide the total by how many numbers you had, and presto! You have your average. Such an easy concept, but ETS decided to make things a bit more difficult.

3

If the average (arithmetic mean) of x, $4x$, and $7x$ is 8, what is the value of x ?

A) 1
B) 2
C) 3
D) 4

What is weird about this question? The question gives you the average! You're dropped off at the end and forced to work backwards. The key to solving average questions it to

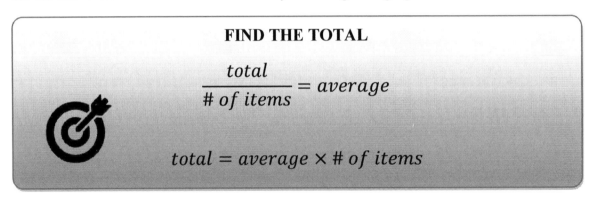

FIND THE TOTAL

$$\frac{total}{\# \ of \ items} = average$$

$$total = average \times \# \ of \ items$$

We can figure out how to do that by reworking the traditional average formula:

Once we have the total, the other quantities should fall into place pretty quickly.

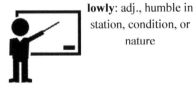

lowly: adj., humble in station, condition, or nature

5

S is a set of numbers whose average (arithmetic mean) is 4. T is a set that is generated by doubling each number in S. What is the average of the numbers in set T ?

A) $\frac{1}{4}$

B) 2

C) 4

D) 8

16

The average (arithmetic mean) weight of 6 pumpkins in a pile is 12 pounds. Another pumpkin is added, and the average weight of the pumpkins in the pile increases to 14 pounds. What is the weight, in pounds, of the added pumpkin?

8

John, Larry, and Dan own a total of 156 marbles. If John owns 46 of them, what is the average (arithmetic mean) number of marbles owned by Larry and Dan?

A) 49

B) 51

C) 53

D) 55

17

The average (arithmetic mean) age of a certain group of 15 employees is 25 years. If 5 additional employees are included in the group, then the average age of the 20 employees is 30 years. What is the average age of the 5 additional employees?

Statistics and Data

Average (Arithmetic Mean)

The issue with average (arithmetic mean) questions is that ACT questions often invert the order in which you're used to solving problems involving averages.

For instance, you'd have no trouble with this question:

However, if the question instead were phrased this way…

3

What's the average of 3, 5, 9, 14, and 19 ?

A) 8
B) 9
C) 10
D) 11

15

The average of 3, 5, x, 14, and 19 is 10. What is the value of x ?

A) 8
B) 9
C) 10
D) 11

…you'd feel much less comfortable. Why?

Because they gave you the average and you're accustomed to being provided the numbers.

Fortunately, this is a easy problem to fix. Just use the FULL equation for arithmetic means:

$$arithmetic\ mean = \frac{sum\ of\ items}{\#\ of\ items}$$

You're always going to be give two of these three components. Use them in the equation above.

24

The mean of 4 numbers is 28. The smallest of the 4 numbers is 6. What is the mean of the other 3 numbers?

A) $30\frac{3}{4}$
B) 32
C) $35\frac{1}{3}$
D) $51\frac{2}{3}$

Median

The median is simply the item in the middle of a list of numbers when they're listed in order. If there are an even number of items in the list, the median is the average of the middle two terms. If you're dealing with a frequency distribution table or histogram, *write out the numbers.*

If you're dealing with a frequency distribution table or a histogram and the question asks about mean or median, do this:

Data Value	Number of Occurrences
1	3
2	5
3	2
4	7

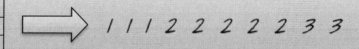

1 1 1 2 2 2 2 2 3 3

14

At a certain location, low tide was measured in inches above (positive) or below (negative) normal sea level for each of 7 consecutive days. The measurements are -2in, 4in, -3in, 1in, 2in, -5in, and -6in. What was the median measurement of these low tide readings?

A) -2in
B) -1in
C) 1in
D) 3in

29

Number of Dreams Remembered	Number of Respondents
0	2
1	6
2	1
3	4
4	2
5 or more	1

The table above contains data recorded from a sleep study. Sixteen participants were asked to record the number of dreams they remember over an 8-hour observation period. What is the median number of dreams participants indicated they remembered during the study?

A) 1
B) 1.5
C) 2
D) 2.5

Mode

Nobody cares about mode. Shut up, mode.

Standard Deviation

Here's the formula you can use to calculate standard deviation:

$$\sigma = \sqrt{\frac{\sum (x - \mu)^2}{N}}$$

for a population, but if you're dealing with the standard deviation of a sample, use…

$$s = \sqrt{\frac{\sum (x - \bar{x})^2}{n - 1}}$$

Got all that? No? Good, because we're just kidding. You don't have to memorize any of that. On the SAT, the most you'll need to know about standard deviation is how it is used to described a set of numbers.

Standard Deviation refers to a how closely grouped around the mean a set of numbers is.

✓ The more *spread out* a set of numbers is, the *greater* the standard deviation.
✓ The more *tightly grouped* a set of numbers is, the *lower* the standard deviation.

Smaller Standard Deviation	Larger Standard Deviation
4, 6, 7, 7, 7, 7, 7, 9	3, 5, 7, 9, 11, 13, 15

22

The tables below give the distribution of peak recorded wind speeds for two mountains (Mountain A and Mountain B) over a 19-day period.

Mountain A

Wind Speed (mph)	Frequency
10	2
20	12
30	3
40	1
50	1

Mountain B

Wind Speed (mph)	Frequency
10	4
20	6
30	3
40	3
50	3

Which of the following is true about the data shown for these 19 days?

A) The standard deviation of maximum wind speeds on Mountain A is larger.
B) The standard deviation of maximum wind speeds on Mountain B is larger.
C) The standard deviation of maximum wind speeds on Mountain A is the same as that of Mountain B.
D) The standard deviation of maximum wind speeds on these mountains cannot be determined with the information provided.

23

Scatterplots of four different data sets are shown below. Which data set displays data with the *smallest* standard deviation?

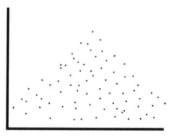

A)

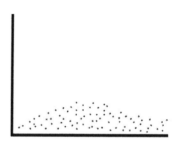

B)

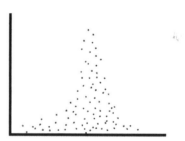

C)

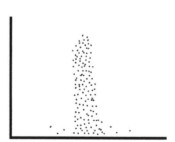

D)

Reading a Pie Chart

A pie chart question is really just a percent or angle question in disguise, so there's no new content here. However, it's a good idea to know how to go back and forth between central angles and percentages.

Just remember: 100% and 360° both represent an entire circle.

How to Convert a Pie Chart Percent into a Central Angle

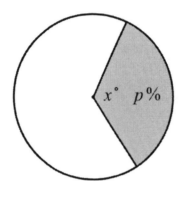

$$\frac{x}{360} = \frac{p}{100}$$

Example:

A wedge in a pie chart represents 35% of the total. What is the central angle measurement of the wedge in degrees?

$$\frac{x}{360} = \frac{35}{100} \qquad \leftarrow \text{Cross multiply}$$

$$100x = 35 \times 360 \qquad \leftarrow \text{Solve for } x$$

$$x = 126 \qquad \text{Tada!}$$

13

Hillary's Monthly Expenses

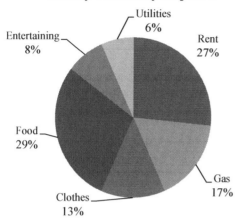

The circle graph above shows Hillary's monthly expenses. If Hillary's total monthly expenses equaled $1,500, in how many categories did she spend less than $300 ?

Bonus Question: On the circle graph above, what is the degree measure of the angle marked with "Gas"?

_____

Probability

Answering a probability question on the SAT is almost always as simple as finding two numbers.

Definition of Probability

$$Probability = \frac{\# \ of \ events \ that \ fulfill \ requirement}{total \ number \ of \ possible \ outcomes}$$

That's it. Find two numbers: the numerator, which represents the number of outcomes that you're seeking, and the denominator, which represents the number of total possible outcomes.

4

There are exactly 9 jelly beans in a jar. There are 4 grape jelly beans and 3 cherry jelly beans, and the rest are lemon. If one jelly bean is drawn at random from the jar, what is the probability that the jelly bean is lemon?

A) $\frac{1}{9}$

B) $\frac{1}{7}$

C) $\frac{2}{9}$

D) $\frac{2}{7}$

8

Sara is getting ready for work. Of the socks in her dresser, 6 pairs are brown. She will randomly pick one pair of the socks to wear. If the probability is $\frac{2}{5}$ that the pair she will pick is brown, how many pairs of socks are in her dresser?

16

$A: \{2, 6, 8, 12, 24, 32\}$

Each number in list A above is multiplied by 4, and this new list of six numbers is called list B. If a number is to be chosen at random from list A, what is the probability that the number chosen will also be in list B ?

Very rarely, the SAT will give you the probability and ask you to find the actual numbers that go into it. Just use the definition provided above.

The Importance of Terminology

Certain words are going to trip you up if you don't know their exact definitions. Here's a list of the most common offenders.

Math Term	Definition
axis	the vertical or horizontal line that divides a coordinate plane; a reference line (e.g., "axis of reflection" is the line across which a reflection takes place)
axes	plural of axis
bisect	to divide into two congruent parts
diameter	the line segment joining two points on a circle and passing through the center of the circle
equilateral	equal sides
equivalent	equal (e.g., equivalent fractions reduce to the same number)
factor	an integer that goes evenly into another integer; one of two or more expressions that are multiplied together to get a product
inclusive	including the endpoints of an interval (e.g., "the interval from 1 to 2, inclusive" means the interval from 1 to 2 including 1 and 2)
inscribe	to draw the largest possible shape within another shape
integer	the set of numbers containing zero, the natural numbers, and all the negatives of the natural numbers
interval	the set of all real numbers between two given numbers; the difference between two successive terms in a sequence
maximum	the highest point in a particular section of a graph
minimum	the lowest point in a particular section of a graph
nonadjacent	not next to
overlap	a portion of area that is shared by two or more geometric shapes
parabola	u-shaped curve that has a focus and is symmetrical about an axis of symmetry
perpendicular	two lines are perpendicular if the angle between them is 90 degrees
polygon	a closed plane figure made up of several line segments that are joined together
precede	to come before
prime (number)	a number whose only factors are itself and 1 (note: 1 is NOT prime)
prism	a solid with parallel congruent bases which are both polygons
radii	plural of radius
reflection	a transformation resulting from a flip
regular	a type of polygon in which all sides are equal and all angles are congruent
tangent	touching at exactly one point; a tangent line touches a curve at a point without crossing over
term	parts of an expression or series separated by + or − signs, or the parts of a sequence separated by commas
vertex	the point on an angle where the two sides intersect
vertices	plural of vertex

159

SAT Reading

Why don't you like the Reading Section?

Think about this question for a while. Imagine yourself taking the test. What characteristics of the test give you the most trouble? Write them out here:

How do you currently approach Passage-Based Reading questions?

Write out the strategy you're currently using, from when you first begin a passage to when you fill in the answer sheet:

Why Everyone Doesn't Like the Reading Section

✓ **Subjectivity** – This isn't like the Math section. On math, once you know that $x = 4$, you go down to the answer choices and circle the appropriate answer choice. On reading, however, you can have a pretty clear idea of the answer and still not get the question correct. Oftentimes, more than one answer choice will feel valid.

✓ **Vocabulary** – On the SAT you're occasionally going to see word you don't know. Knowing the words that are likely to appear on the test will make a HUGE difference in your score.

✓ **Tough Passages** – While test-takers will never be expected to read above grade level on the SAT, some of the passages can be daunting. The author can have an especially nuanced argument or use *abstruse* language. Getting through these passages can be a struggle.

✓ **Boring Passages** – It's safe to say that a typical student wouldn't voluntarily read most of the passages on the test.

How to Do Better

✓ Have a Reliable Strategy
✓ Know the Question Types
✓ Know Your Vocabulary
✓ Know What the Test Makers Expect
✓ Speak for Yourself
✓ Use Context

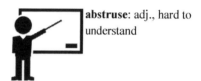

abstruse: adj., hard to understand

The technique for Critical Reading questions is quite easy to learn. Once you master the techniques, you'll understand how the test makers try to manipulate you.

Order of Difficulty

Critical Reading questions DO NOT follow order of difficulty. Easier and more difficult questions will be intermingled; you can jump around a bit more on these questions.

Critical Reading Approach

Step 1: Read the Italicized Introduction
- Provides a brief snapshot of text
- Provides context
- Helps gauge level of interest

Step 2: Read the Passage
- Read at comfortable pace
- Take *brief* notes if you're having trouble focusing

Step 3: Brief Analysis
- What type of passage is it?
    - Narrative: Who are the characters? What do they do and say? Why?
    - Expository: What is the passage about? How does the author characterize that?
    - Persuasive: What is the author selling? How does he try to do it?

Step 4: Question Selection
- Tackle more specific questions first. Save broader questions for later.
- Ensure you understand the question. Is it a literal comprehension or authorial intent question?

Step 5: Go Back to the Passage
- If there is a line reference, read more than the lines suggested. The answer is typically in the adjacent text. If you understand the text, you'll know when you have found the answer.
- If there is no line reference, check to see whether the question is an "Answer, then Support" type of question.

Step 6: Answer in Your Own Words (if possible)
- Before you go to the answer choices, you have to know what you're looking for.
- Be sure your answer is directly supported by the text.

Step 7: Use Process of Elimination
- Eliminate Answer Choices that don't match what you said in step 6.
- Eliminate Answer Choices that aren't directly supported by the text.
- Eliminate Answer Choices that don't answer the question being asked.
- Eliminate Answer Choices that look good but have a minor flaw.
- Choose the remaining Answer Choice.

How to Deal with the Answer Choices

This isn't math. Things aren't so black and white. You're going to need to have a consistent approach toward evaluating the Answer Choices to systematically identify the correct answer.

- If the Answer Choice *is a really close match to your answer*, put a check next to it. Heck, put two checks if you really love it. DO NOT circle it immediately. You may find another answer you like more.
- If the Answer Choice *has nothing to do with your answer*, cross it out. Stick to your guns.
- If the Answer Choice *is just ok (you don't love it, but you don't hate it)*, put a "w" next to it to label it a weak answer.
- If the Answer Choice *is indecipherable*, put a question mark next to it. **DO NOT CROSS IT OUT.**

Every single Answer Choice should have one of these four ratings next to it. Your test should look something like this:

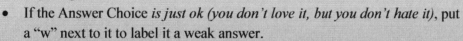

14

He was emotional eating

The passage suggests that Dan regrets eating the entire pizza because:

  ✗ F. he didn't know about the unlimited breadsticks.

  w G. he made a promise to himself to stick to five slices.

  ? H. overeating was a sublimation of his inner inadequacies.

  ✗ J. there wasn't adequate food for his coworkers.

When you're honest with yourself about the Answer Choices, your life becomes so much easier.

What do you think the student should do on the question above?

Expository Passages

Passages will come in three different writing styles: **Expository, Persuasive** and **Narrative**.

Expository Passages

- The author wants to characterize something.
- Tone is generally interested or enthusiastic.
- Questions will focus on characterization.

Since expository passages require the author to characterize something in a clear, compelling way, the questions will focus on how the author describes the subject of the passage.

Examples of Questions that Accompany Expository Passages

✓ "The passage is primarily concerned with…"
✓ "In the passage, <something> serves as an example of…"
✓ "The author mentions <something> to emphasize…"
✓ "The discussion of <something> most directly demonstrates…"
✓ "The author lists <something> primarily in order to…"
✓ "What best describes the function of line <number>?"
✓ "The statement signals a shift from…"
✓ "Which generalization about <something> is most supported by the passage?"
✓ "The paragraph describes all of the following EXCEPT…"

Do you see how the questions focus on description? Keep that in mind when you're working through the following questions.

 emphatic: adj., uttered, or to be uttered, with emphasis; strongly expressive; forceful

The following passage is adapted from an essay about the history of the electric car. The author considers possible reasons for the electric car's slow ascension to popularity in the United States.

The story of the electric car serves as a tale of corporate activism and the nature of innovation. The recent rise in sales and visibility of hybrid fuel and fully electric cars belies the fact that the technology
5 has actually existed before conventional internal combustion engine-powered automobiles. The first electric car was built by an American inventor in 1834, right around the time when Andrew Jackson was censured by Congress and Athens became the
10 capital of Greece.

Electric cars were quite popular in the U.S. in the late 19th and early 20th centuries; they provided ease of use and a level of comfort that wasn't then possible with more primitive internal combustion
15 engines – electric vehicles didn't have the vibration, smell, or noise normally associated with gasoline cars. Starting a gasoline-powered car required the user to turn a hand crank attached to the engine, a dangerous task that often resulted in injury. So
20 popular was the electric vehicle that there were proposals as early as 1896 for the creation of an electric infrastructure to provide for battery exchanges for car users. In 1897, a fleet of electric taxis travelled the streets of New York City.

25 Advance s in gasoline-powered cars and mass production quickly eroded those advantages and allowed sales of gasoline powered vehicles to outpace those of their electric counterparts. Increased comfort, better driving range and greater speeds
30 became major selling points. Gasoline prices went down with an increase in oil refineries. And an electric starter made the gasoline car much easier to use. Additionally, limitations in battery storage stifled innovation in electric car design. The internal
35 combustion engine quickly gained momentum with Henry Ford's Model T, which gave consumers what they wanted in a reliable and inexpensive package.

The gasoline car's dominance continued for nearly 80 years. High gasoline prices in the 1960's
40 and 1970's resulted in a brief reemergence of electric cars. In the 1990's, General Motors created the EV1, which was the topic of the 2006 documentary *Who Killed the Electric Car?* The filmmakers argue that

the oil industry and major car companies colluded to
45 delay the installation of public car charging stations and eliminate the need for higher government-mandated fuel efficiency standards. Marketing campaigns also shaped public perception of the electric cars to ensure supply outpaced demand.
50 These efforts depressed consumer demand and thus discouraged production of electric cars.

Unsurprisingly, more recent increases in gasoline prices and political turmoil in many oil-producing countries have renewed interest in fuel-efficient
55 vehicles, which include hybrid, alternative fuel, and fully electric models. The Toyota Prius, the first mass-produced hybrid vehicle, is now sold in more than 80 countries, and the Nissan Leaf and Tesla Roadster, both totally electric cars, are beginning to
60 gain market share and increase awareness. Perhaps we're now learning that certain innovations cannot be contained when their time has come.

Ask yourself these questions when you're reading the passage:

Why did the author write this passage?

_____

_____

_____

What is the main idea of the passage?

_____

_____

_____

How is the main topic characterized in the passage?

_____

_____

_____

Narrative Passages

Passages will come in three different writing styles: **Narrative**, **Expository**, and **Persuasive**.

Narrative Passages

- The author wants to tell a compelling story.
- Tone will depend on the plot.
- Questions will focus on narrative elements.

Since narrative passages require the author to tell a story in a compelling way or paint a vivid picture of a character, most of the questions will focus on storytelling devices and narrative elements (if it's a plot-driven story) or character analysis (if it's a character study).

Examples of Questions that Accompany Narrative Passages

- ✓ "The rhetorical device in the passage is…"
- ✓ "The lines are notable for their…"
- ✓ "The episode in the passage is best described as…"
- ✓ "The lines suggest <a character> is motivated by…"
- ✓ "<Character 1> and <Character 2> would most likely agree on which point?"
- ✓ "The character's use of the words/actions is best described as…"
- ✓ "The character reacts by…"
- ✓ "The character's attitude is best described as…"
- ✓ "What does the description suggest about the character?"
- ✓ "The imagery serves to convey the…"

Do you see how the questions focus on what's going on in the story and how the author is moving things along? Keep that in mind when you're reading the following passage.

The following passage is adapted from a short story about a doctor and his friend.

Mrs. Hudson, the landlady of my friend, was a long-suffering woman. Not only was her first-floor flat invaded at all hours by throngs of singular and often undesirable characters but her remarkable

5 lodger showed an eccentricity and irregularity in his life which must have sorely tried her patience. His incredible untidiness, his addiction to music at strange hours, his occasional revolver practice within doors, his weird and often malodorous scientific

10 experiments, and the atmosphere of violence and danger which hung around him made him the very worst tenant in London. On the other hand, his payments were princely. I have no doubt that the house might have been purchased at the price which

15 Holmes paid for his rooms during the years that I was with him.

The landlady stood in the deepest awe of him and never dared to interfere with him, however outrageous his proceedings might seem. She was

20 fond of him, too, for he had a remarkable gentleness and courtesy in his dealings with women. He disliked and distrusted the gender, but he was always a chivalrous opponent. Knowing how genuine was her regard for him, I listened earnestly to her story when

25 she came to my rooms in the second year of my married life and told me of the sad condition to which my poor friend was reduced.

"He's dying, Dr. Watson," said she. "For three days he has been sinking, and I doubt if he will last

30 the day. He would not let me get a doctor. This morning when I saw his bones sticking out of his face and his great bright eyes looking at me I could stand no more of it. 'With your leave or without it, Mr. Holmes, I am going for a doctor this very hour,' said

35 I. 'Let it be Watson, then,' said he. I wouldn't waste an hour in coming to him, sir, or you may not see him alive."

I was horrified for I had heard nothing of his illness. I need not say that I rushed for my coat and

40 my hat. As we drove back I asked for the details.

"There is little I can tell you, sir. He has been working at a case down at a lab in an alley near the river, and he has brought this illness back with him. He took to his bed on Wednesday afternoon and has

45 never moved since. For these three days neither food nor drink has passed his lips."

"Good God! Why did you not call in a doctor?"

"He wouldn't have it, sir. You know how masterful he is. I didn't dare to disobey him. But he's

50 not long for this world, as you'll see for yourself the moment that you set eyes on him."

Ask yourself these questions when you're reading the passage.

Who are the characters?

_____

_____

_____

_____

What happens?

_____

_____

_____

_____

What do the characters think about the events?

_____

_____

_____

_____

167

Persuasive Passages

Passages will come in three different writing styles: **Persuasive**, **Expository**, and **Narrative**.

Persuasive Passages

- The author has an argument to sell.
- Tone is generally emphatic or *exasperated*.
- Questions will focus on rhetoric.

Since persuasive passages require the author to try to convince the reader of the validity of a certain point of view, most of the questions will focus on how the author tries to get his or her point across to the reader.

Examples of Questions that Accompany Persuasive Passages

- ✓ "The author of the passage would most likely…"
- ✓ "The observation establishes a contrast between…"
- ✓ "The author makes which point about…"
- ✓ "The author of the passage would probably agree/disagree…"
- ✓ "The author <does something> in order to…"
- ✓ "The reference <to something> serves primarily to…"
- ✓ "The author's tone/tone of the passage is…"
- ✓ "The author would likely respond <to something> with…"

Do you see how the questions tend to focus on the author? Keep that in mind when you're working through the following passage.

exasperated: adj., irritated or provoked to a high degree

The following passage discusses the origins or potential shortcomings of a particular political process.

There are a distressing number of traditions observed in the United States that have become obsolete and thus deserve honest reevaluation. Many of these traditions have their origins in agrarian
5 considerations that are no longer significant. The country's continued observation of these archaic traditions speaks volumes about its reluctance to improve efficiency. Perhaps the people should consider the costs invoked by blind devotion to
10 policies that have outlived their usefulness.

Consider voting. In 1792, federal law chose November as a desirable month for elections because the harvest would have been completed and winter storms would not have begun. Tuesday was chosen
15 as the best day of the week because farmers needed a full day to travel by horse-drawn vehicle to the county seat to vote. "Why not Wednesday?", you might ask. Well, the legislators also wanted to avoid interfering with the Biblical Sabbath or with many
20 towns' market day.

The world has changed a lot since then, and many critics of the current electoral system rightly point out that holding elections on Tuesday makes voting much more difficult for the majority of people who work a
25 traditional Monday through Friday, 9am-5pm schedule. Granted, many employers provide an hour or two of paid leave to participate in elections. Unfortunately, the wait to vote in many highly populated areas can often exceed that amount of time.

30 In the United States, there were 2.2 million farmers, representing less than 1% of the total population. Why is such a small constituency offered such deference? Perhaps some of the wire-pullers benefit from the potential disenfranchisement that
35 this schedule engenders.

Reformers have suggested several correctives. The most obvious solution is to move Election Day to a weekend, when the majority of Americans aren't working. Another proposal involves making Election
40 Day a federal holiday, thus allowing people who normally work on Tuesdays to vote at their convenience. Lastly, some activists have proposed allowing the process to occur over several days instead of just one.

45 Defenders of the current practice assert that alternate means of voting – such as mail-in voting or early voting – are readily available to citizens who struggle to participate in the traditional arrangement. They often argue that big changes to the system will
50 produce unwelcome difficulties. However, when one considers the origins of undeniably inconvenient practices, it might be time to rethink the current policies.

Ask yourself these questions when you're reading the passage.

What is the author's argument?

_____
_____
_____
_____

How does he make his point?

_____
_____
_____
_____

How convincing is he? Why?

_____
_____
_____
_____

Literal Comprehension

Critical Reading questions come in two broad flavors: **Literal Comprehension** and **Authorial Intent**.

Literal Comprehension Question

- Asks "What does the passage say?"
- Does NOT require reading between the lines
- Contextual clues are closer
- Easier to answer in your own words
- Tests comprehension skills

A **Literal Comprehension** question's difficulty is directly tied to the difficulty of the passage. Keep in mind these guidelines when you're working through these types of questions.

Literal Comprehension Questions Rules

Find Support in the Text: Use the "**Point Test**." If you can't point to the portion of the passage that supports your answer, you're picking the wrong answer.

Don't Read Between the Lines: This bears repeating. Even if the question uses words like "imply", "infer", or "suggest", you're *only* being tested on what's in the passage.

Read for Context: The answer will almost never be where you're told to look. You're going to have to read around the reference.

Answer in Your Own Words: This won't always be possible; do it whenever you can.

...Mrs. Hudson, the landlady of my friend, was a long-suffering woman. Not only was her first-floor flat invaded at all hours by throngs of singular and often undesirable characters but her remarkable lodger showed an eccentricity and irregularity in his life which must have sorely tried her patience. His incredible untidiness, his addiction to music at strange hours, his occasional revolver practice within doors, his weird and often malodorous scientific experiments, and the atmosphere of violence and danger which hung around him made him the very worst tenant in London. On the other hand, his payments were princely. I have no doubt that the house might have been purchased at the price which Holmes paid for his rooms during the years that I was with him...

...Advance s in gasoline-powered cars and mass production quickly eroded those advantages and allowed sales of gasoline powered vehicles to outpace those of their electric counterparts. Increased comfort, better driving range and greater speeds became major selling points. Gasoline prices went down with an increase in oil refineries. And an electric starter made the gasoline car much easier to use. Additionally, limitations in contemporary battery storage technology stifled innovation in electric car design. The internal combustion engine quickly gained momentum with Henry Ford's Model T, which gave consumers what they wanted in a reliable and inexpensive package...

50 ...some defenders of the current practice assert that alternate means of voting – such as mail-in voting or early voting – are readily available to citizens who struggle to participate in the traditional arrangement. They often argue that big changes to the system will
55 produce unwelcome difficulties. However, when one considers the origins of undeniably inconvenient practices, it might be time to rethink the current policies...

16

The passage mentions all of the following as evidence of Holmes's eccentricity EXCEPT

A) his erratic schedule
B) his volatile personality
C) his tendency to make too much noise
D) his effect on other tenant's experiences

19

According to passage, what characteristic of electric cars initially limited the rate of the technology's improvement?

A) prohibitively high prices
B) inadequate technologies then available
C) insufficient popular demand
D) unappealing vehicle aesthetics

21

In line 50, "defenders'" use of "alternate means of voting" are used by as

A) unnecessary attempts to complicate an otherwise efficient system
B) methods that affect certain groups more than others
C) means by which people can participate in political debate
D) deceptive practices that obscure true intentions

Imply, Infer, Conclude, Suggest Questions

Few words strike fear into the hearts of students more than these.

> **Examples of Imply, Infer, Conclude, Suggest Questions**
>
> ✓ "The narrator suggests the character is sometimes…"
> ✓ "The question in lines <#> imply…
> ✓ "What does the description suggest about…"
> ✓ "It can be inferred that the author believes…"
> ✓ "The lines <#> suggest primarily…"

Let's clear things up with an example:

> **Scenario: Patrick enters the room.   His hair is wet.**
>
> **Everyday Life Explanations**
>
> • It must be raining and he forgot an umbrella.
> • He just took a shower.
> • He went for a swim recently.
> • His hair was messy and he tried to fix it.
> • Someone hit him with a water balloon.
>
> **SAT Explanation**
>
> • A liquid has come in contact with his hair and hasn't yet evaporated.

Do you see the difference? We use our everyday understanding of these words on a test that has a very different definition of them.

When you're dealing with these types of questions, stay away from answer choices that COULD be true and stick to the ones that MUST be true.

There are **a lot** of these on the test.

Got it? **Practice.**

SAT READING
PASSAGE BASED QUESTIONS

…Mrs. Hudson, the landlady of my friend, was a long-suffering woman. Not only was her first-floor flat invaded at all hours by throngs of singular and often undesirable characters but her remarkable lodger showed an eccentricity and irregularity in his life which must have sorely tried her patience. His incredible untidiness, his addiction to music at strange hours, his occasional revolver practice within doors, his weird and often malodorous scientific experiments, and the atmosphere of violence and danger which hung around him made him the very worst tenant in London. On the other hand, Holmes's payments were princely…

…As a result, Watterson regularly rejects licensing requests, which would allow outside parties to profit from his artistic endeavors. He is also notoriously averse to granting interviews with the media. Perhaps Watterson understands that true artistic integrity is more a function of a deep desire to produce something personal and less an opportunity to wring every ounce of profit from one's work…

…There is a particular spot within the National Statuary Hall in the United States Capitol that has a somewhat apocryphal history. Known as the "Whisper Spot," the location possesses interesting acoustical properties. The amphitheater dome allows a person standing on a specific floor tile to clearly hear a conversation from the other side of the hall – nearly 200 feet away. It has been said that John Adams took advantage of the Hall's acoustics to surreptitiously eavesdrop on colleagues under the impression their words were confidential…

…Electric cars were quite popular in the U.S. in the late 19th and early 20th centuries; they provided ease of use and a level of comfort that wasn't then possible with more primitive internal combustion engines – electric vehicles didn't have the vibration, smell, or noise normally associated with gasoline cars. So popular was the electric vehicle that there were proposals as early as 1896 for the creation of an electric infrastructure to provide for battery exchanges for car users. In 1897, a fleet of electric taxis travelled the streets of New York City…

12

The discussion of Holmes's habits in lines 11-16 ("His incredible…in London") suggests that

A) Holmes lives a carefree lifestyle
B) Holmes is an inconsiderate person
C) Holmes's habits are disruptive
D) Mrs. Hudson is planning to evict Holmes

17

The discussion in lines 18-25 ("As a result…one's work") primarily suggests that

A) Third parties are interested in using Watterson's work for financial gain
B) Watterson disapproves of artists who license their work
C) Watterson is apprehensive of interaction with the media
D) Watterson is financially successful

19

In lines 26-35 ("There is…confidential"), the author implies

A) The design of the "Whisper Spot" was intentional
B) The origins of the "Whisper Spot" have been intentionally obfuscated
C) John Adams's political opponents had their conversations intercepted
D) There are several stories that explain the creation of the "Whisper Spot"

22

It can be inferred that the American public preferred electric cars to gasoline ones because

A) electric cars were more affordable
B) gasoline vehicles hadn't yet reached a commensurate level of aesthetics
C) the electric car was more readily available
D) electric cars were less difficult to operate

Tone / Attitude

In person, it's really easy to determine a person's tone or attitude. That's because 90% of interpersonal communication is non-verbal. You can hear it in someone's voice or see it in her body language. When all you have to work with is verbal, you need to do a lot with that 10%.

Luckily, there are only a few places to look for the tone.

How to Find Tone

✓ Look for descriptive language. The author's choice of adjectives and adverbs will tell you how he feels about something.

✓ Use the words' *connotations*. Words can have the same denotation but vastly different connotations.

  o *I would like to speak with my mother.* vs. *I would like to speak with my mommy.*

✓ Consider what topics the author chooses to focus on. Are they negative or positive?

✓ If all else fails, go with humorous. If you're not getting the joke, the passage will feel toneless.

 connotation: noun. an idea or feeling that a word invokes in addition to its literal or primary meaning

 denotation: noun. the literal or primary meaning of a word, in contrast to the feelings or ideas that the word suggests

There are a distressing number of traditions observed in the United States that have become obsolete and thus deserve honest reevaluation. Many of these traditions have their origins in agrarian
5 considerations that are no longer significant. The country's continued observation of these archaic traditions speaks volumes about its reluctance to improve efficiency. Perhaps the people should consider the costs invoked by blind devotion to
10 policies that have outlived their usefulness.

10

The author's attitude towards certain "traditions" (line 1) can best be described as

A) puzzlement
B) skepticism
C) bemusement
D) anger

…An absolute monarchy is one in which the sovereign does as he pleases so long as he pleases the assassins. Not many absolute monarchies are left, most of them having been replaced by limited monarchies, where the sovereign's power for evil (and for good) is greatly curtailed, and by republics, which are governed by chance…

25

The author's tone can best be characterized as

A) sanctimonious
B) wry
C) contemptuous
D) emphatic

Rhetorical Devices

The SAT will occasionally ask you to describe the author's use of language with strictly defined literary terms. Since that makes the problems essentially vocabulary questions, a review of the terminology is in order.

> **Note:** This list is LOW PRIORITY. You'll see maybe one or two of these questions per tests. However, if you're shooting for a high score (700+), you must memorize this list.

Term	Meaning
Abstract	Not related to the concrete properties of an object; pertaining to ideas, concepts, or qualities, as opposed to physical attributes.
Aesthetic	Pertaining to the value of art for its own sake or for form.
Allegory	Narrative form in which characters and actions have meanings outside themselves; characters are usually personifications of abstract qualities.
Alliteration	The repetition of initial consonant sounds or any vowel sounds within a formal grouping, such as a poetic line or stanza, or in close proximity in prose.
Allusion	A figure of speech which makes brief, even casual reference to a historical or literary figure, event, or object to create a resonance in the reader or to apply a symbolic meaning to the character or object of which the allusion consists.
Ambiguity	Use of language in which multiple meanings are possible. Ambiguity can be unintentional through insufficient focus on the part of the writer; in good writing, ambiguity is frequently intentional in the form of multiple connotative meanings, or situations in which either the connotative or the denotative meaning can be valid in a reading.
Anachronism	Use of historically inaccurate details in a text; for example, depicting a 19th-century character using a computer.
Analogy	Comparison of two things that are alike in some respects. Metaphors and similes are both types of analogy.
Anecdote	A brief story or tale told by a character in a piece of literature.
Audience	The person(s) reached by a piece of writing.
Catharsis	Purification or cleansing of the spirit through the emotions of pity and terror as a witness to a tragedy.
Connotation	What is implied by a word. For example, the words sweet, gay, and awesome have connotations that are quite different from their actual definitions.
Contradiction	A direct opposition between things compared; inconsistency.
Denotation	The dictionary definition of a word; the direct and specific meaning.
Diction	An author's choice of words to convey a tone or effect.
Didactic	Intended for teaching or to teach a moral lesson.
Eulogy	A speech or writing in praise of a person or thing; an oration in honor of a deceased person.
Euphemism	Substitution of a milder or less direct expression for one that is harsh or blunt.
Foreshadow	To hint at or present things to come in a story or play.
Formal Language	Language that is lofty.
Genre	Term used to describe literary forms, such as tragedy, comedy, novel, or essay.
Hyperbole	An overstatement characterized by exaggerated language.

Term	Meaning
Imagery	Sensory details in a work; the use of figurative language to evoke a feeling, call to mind an idea, or describe an object. Imagery involves any or all of the five senses.
Irony	A situation or statement characterized by significant difference between what is expected or understood and what actually happens or is meant. Irony is frequently humorous.
Juxtaposition	Placing of two items side by side to create a certain effect, reveal an attitude, or accomplish some other purpose.
Mood	The feeling or ambience resulting from the tone of a piece as well as the writer/narrator's attitude and point of view. The effect is created through descriptions of feelings or objects that establish a particular feeling such as gloom, fear, or hope.
Motif	Recurrent device, formula, or situation that often serves as a signal for the appearance of a character or event.
Nostalgia	Desire to return in thought or fact to a former time.
Oxymoron	A figure of speech that combines two apparently contradictory elements, as in "jumbo shrimp" or "deafening silence."
Paradox	A statement that seems contradictory, but is actually true.
Parody	A satirical imitation of a work of art for purpose of ridiculing its style or subject.
Personification	Treating an abstraction or nonhuman object as if it were a person by giving it human qualities.
Perspective	A character's view of the situation or events in the story.
Point of view	The view the reader gets of the action and characters in a story
Propaganda	Information or rumor deliberately spread to help or harm a person, group, or institution.
Protagonist	The chief character in a work of literature.
Sarcasm	A sharp caustic remark. A form of verbal irony in which apparent praise is actually bitterly or harshly critical.
Satire	A literary style used to make fun of or ridicule an idea or human vice or weakness.
Syntax	The way words are put together to form phrases, clauses, and sentences. It is sentence structure and how it influences the way a reader perceives a piece of writing.
Theme	The central or dominant idea or concern of a work; the main idea or meaning.
Thesis	Focus statement of an essay; premise statement upon which the point of view or discussion in the essay is based.
Tone	A speech or writing in praise of a person or thing; an oration in honor of a deceased person.
Transition words	Words and devices that bring unity and coherence to a piece of writing.

If you know the definitions, answering the questions become quite straightforward.

…Her voice was a whip. Each word a vicious crack across my back as she pointed out my shortcomings…

… He remembered the smells of his mother's kitchen. He would often wonder how she could combine such pedestrian ingredients to produce such wondrous creations. In his apartment, as he slowly stirred a pot of bland noodles, he wished he had paid more attention…

…the tea kettle hissed and screamed, begging us for attention…

16

The author uses which of the following in lines 16-18 ?

A) personification
B) analogy
C) metaphor
D) parody

18

The tone of lines 22-27 can best be described as

A) ironic
B) dour
C) nostalgic
D) oppressive

20

In line 42, the writing can best be described as displaying

(A) personification
(B) hyperbole
(C) allegory
(D) juxtaposition

Rhetoric

Broadly, rhetoric refers to the means by which someone attempts to persuade someone else. While there are literally dozens of methods for doing this, the SAT tends to use passages that rely on only a few.

Name	Description	Example
Quoting Authorities	The author has scientists, scholars, or experts give their opinions on the subject.	"Thurston Howell indicates as much in his recent study, where he…"
Correlation	The author uses the idea that if A (or lack thereof) usually precedes or accompanies B, A probably causes B.	"The number of pirates in the world has steadily decreased, while average global temperatures have increased. Coincidence?"
Attacking the Opposition	The author implies that no reasonable person would believe the opposing viewpoint.	"To argue that there aren't socialists in our government is naïve."
Common Sense	The author argues that his thesis is merely an application of common sense.	"Obviously, soda isn't good for you. It's so obvious a law restricting its use is unnecessary."
Analogy	The author uses an example that shares characteristics with whatever his argument is about.	"If a single payer health care system can work in Canada, surely it could also work in this country."
Bandwagon	The author appeals to the reader's inclination to conform to a larger group.	"You should try marijuana because over 50% of Americans have tried it."
Anti-Bandwagon	The author indicates that a common definition or conceptualization is wrong and only experts know the truth.	"Many people believe there is a scary man in the sky that watches their every move. These people are wrong."

What types of rhetoric are the authors using in the following passages?

Proponents of gun control legislation should remember the failed war on drugs in the late 20th century in the United States; banning illegal drugs hasn't done much to diminish their usage.

Critics of violence in video games should remember one very important point: it is impossible to shoot someone with a virtual firearm. This is de facto proof that video games don't cause violence.

The case for the efficacy of alternative medicine is relatively clear cut. 7 in 10 doctors say acupuncture works; therefore it must work.

The historian Dean Keith Simonton, who researches the factors involved in musical and literary creativity, especially Shakespeare's, concludes "beyond a shadow of a doubt" that the consensus play chronology is roughly the correct order, and that Shakespeare's works exhibit gradual stylistic development consistent with that of other artistic geniuses. This suggests that the mystery surrounding Shakespeare's identify is merely the product of overly imaginative literary sleuths.

Main Idea

Strictly speaking, main idea questions ask "What is the passage about?" Because the SAT cares more about your ability to read critically than to summarize, these questions are pretty rare.

The SAT makes "main idea" questions more difficult in two main ways:

- ✓ The Main Idea question is the first question after the passage.
- ✓ The Answer Choices contain answers that are correct, but too specific.

On Main Idea Questions…

- ✓ Complete the other questions first. You'll have a more complete understanding of the Main Idea after you answer the rest of the questions. Save the Main Idea question for last.
- ✓ Eliminate Answer Choices that focus on only one portion of the passage, even if they're accurate.

They're pretty rare, so don't be surprised if you don't see one. Keep this advice in mind on the following question.

The following passage considers the impact of a country's political and cultural history on methods of expression.

The term "political unconscious" refers to those things that are so ingrained in our culture that we do not consider them political or cultural, although they are. Because we, as members of a culture, work within the confines of our "political unconscious," any narrative we may produce will be produced in accordance with our culture's "master narrative." The underlying implications of this idea provide a theoretical backdrop for the more specific theories of gender and race. Thus there is an underlying cultural force that molds our discourse and our literature. Culture supplants nature in the formation of literature and discourse, and in the consequent formation of our cultural and personal identities.

The only effective liberation from such constraints begins with the recognition that there is nothing that is not social and historical – indeed, that everything is political. Thus, what constrains us is the fallacy that our basic assumptions are not a product of our culture and our membership in it, but are in some way naturally generated. Everything is political because it is culturally rather than naturally constructed, and our interpretation of literature and discourse functions within the confines of these constructs and must be read as such. Not only must we interpret the literature of a culture from a "political perspective," but also we must see all literature as a reflection of the culture's "master narrative."

In her essay, "Playing in the Dark," Toni Morrison[1] argues that the black presence in America is a defining feature of American literature and identity, though it has not previously been acknowledged as such. The "Africanist presence," as Morrison calls it, is vital to the formation of the identity, and thus the literature, that is specific to America.

She writes, "The concept of freedom did not emerge in a vacuum. Nothing highlighted freedom – if it did not in fact create it – like slavery.". The American dream of freedom and ownership, of democracy could not have been established without the visible presence of the lack of freedom, ownership, and democracy, which the slaves provided. This dream shaped the identity of the white American. Thus, for Morrison, the creation of America's "master narrative" is dependent on what is superficially excluded from it. Morrison definitively states that: "The very manner by which American literature distinguishes itself as a coherent entity exists because of this unsettled and unsettling population." In other words, the presence of black slaves and their freed descendants is what makes the American canon uniquely American.

These theories are particularly useful in the analysis and understanding of our culture's literature within a cultural context. In her work as a literary theorist and writer, Morrison turns an analytical eye on her constraints as a writer within the highly categorized world in which we live. Beyond the context of literary analysis, Morrison calls attention to the fact that our culture is dominated by these culturally constructed groups and categories. The result of this, however, is somewhat paradoxical. Though they give us the tools to rethink and reform the very way in which we perceive our own identities, they also reveal the great extent to which our culture has the power to define and confine us.

17

Which of the following expresses the main idea of the passage?

A) Toni Morrison is a tireless critic of the American cultural zeitgeist.
B) A nation's past can have a profound impact on cultural and artistic themes.
C) Narrative themes are predetermined by one's surroundings.
D) Literature is often country specific.

---

[1] Toni Morrison (1931-) is an American novelist, editor, and professor.

Authorial Intent

Critical Reading questions come in two broad flavors: **Literal Comprehension** and **Authorial Intent.**

Authorial Intent Question

- Asks "Why did the author write that?"
- Does NOT require reading between the lines
- Contextual clues are more dispersed
- Harder to answer in your own words
- Tests Critical Reading skills

An **Authorial Intent** question's difficulty is directly tied to the complexity and subtlety of the author's position. Keep in mind these guidelines when you're working through these types of questions.

Authorial Intent Questions Rules

Find Support in the Text: Use the "Point Test." If you can't point to the portion of the passage that supports your answer, you're picking the wrong answer.

Use the Purpose: Ask yourself, "Does this answer choice agree with the passage's main idea or purpose?" A correct answer will agree with the main idea.

Read for Context: Authorial Intent questions are much more contextually driven, so you're going to have to look for context clues sometimes very far away from the reference in the questions.

Answer in Your Own Words: This won't always be possible; do it whenever you can.

15 ...Electric cars were quite popular in the U.S. in the late 19th and early 20th centuries; they provided ease of use and a level of security that wasn't then possible with more primitive internal combustion engines – electric vehicles didn't have the vibration,
20 smell, or noise normally associated with gasoline cars. Starting a gasoline-powered car required the user to turn a hand crank attached to the engine, a dangerous task that often resulted in injury. So popular was the electric vehicle that there were
25 proposals as early as 1896 for the creation of an electric infrastructure to provide for battery exchanges for car users. In 1897, a fleet of electric taxis travelled the streets of New York City...

17

In paragraph 3, the author lists all of the following as advantages of electric cars over gasoline cars EXCEPT

A) superior aesthetics
B) greater comfort
C) simplicity of operation
D) greater availability

18

The author mentions the "fleet of electric taxis" (line 27) in order to

A) offer evidence to support a previous assertion
B) dramatize as set of circumstances
C) emphasize a change in motivations
D) contradict a common assumption

Primary Purpose

Purpose questions are directly linked to Authorial Intent. These questions ask "WHY did the author say that?" and **not** "WHAT did the author say?"

How to Recognize "Primary Purpose" Questions

- The question uses the word "primary" or "primarily." Duh.

The key to answering these questions is generally a function of the type of passage you're on.

- For **Expository Passages**, the purpose will be related to helping the author describe or characterize something.
- For **Narrative Passages**, the purpose will be related to moving the plot forward, explaining a character's motivation, or describing a character or plot element.
- For **Persuasive Passages**, the purpose will be related to strengthening the author's argument or weakening an opposing viewpoint. Occasionally, it will be related to making a small *concession* in the argument.

For all Primary Purpose questions, you must remember that the word primary denotes "For more than any other reason." That means if you're stuck with more than one answer choice, go with the one that has more support. More specific answers will be the wrong answers with these types of questions.

 concession: noun, the act of giving up or yielding a point or fact in an argument

...There are a distressing number of traditions observed in the United States that have become obsolete and thus deserve honest reevaluation. Many of these traditions have their origins in agrarian
5 considerations that are no longer significant. The country's continued observation of these archaic traditions speaks volumes about its reluctance to improve efficiency. Perhaps the people should consider the costs invoked by blind devotion to policies that
10 have outlived their usefulness.

Consider voting. In 1792, federal law chose November as a desirable month for elections because the harvest would have been completed and winter storms would not have begun. Tuesday was chosen as
15 the best day of the week because farmers needed a full day to travel by horse-drawn vehicle to the county seat to vote. "Why not Wednesday?" you might ask. Well, the legislators also wanted to avoid interfering with the Biblical Sabbath or with many towns' market days...

20 ...Unsurprisingly, more recent increases in gasoline prices and political turmoil in many oil-producing countries have renewed interest in fuel-efficient vehicles, which include hybrid, alternative fuel, and fully electric models. The Toyota Prius, the first mass-
25 produced hybrid vehicle, is now sold in more than 80 countries, and the Nissan Leaf and Tesla Roadster, both totally electric cars, are beginning to gain market share and increase awareness. Perhaps we're now learning that certain innovations cannot be contained when their
30 time has come...

...The landlady stood in the deepest awe of him and never dared to interfere with him, however outrageous
35 his proceedings might seem. She was fond of him, too, for he had a remarkable gentleness and courtesy in his dealings with women. He disliked and distrusted the gender, but he was always a chivalrous opponent. Knowing how genuine was her regard for him, I
40 listened earnestly to her story when she came to my rooms in the second year of my married life and told me of the sad condition to which my poor friend was reduced...

12

The first paragraph primarily serves to

A) provide a common argument the author later refutes
B) defend a contemporary practice
C) provide context for subsequent discussion
D) establish the foundation for an emotional plea

22

The author mentions the "gasoline prices and political turmoil" (line 24) primarily to

A) offer possible explanations for the reemergence of electric vehicles
B) provide a historical narrative for the discussion
C) detail critical elements of car production
D) cast doubts on reasons behind a recent development

27

The primary purpose of lines 38-42 ("She was...opponent") is to

A) characterize an interpersonal relationship
B) create a tension between two characters
C) consider a factor in a person's motivation
D) explain a paradox

Interpret the Reference

This is the most common type of question on the Critical Reading portion of the SAT. Interpret the Reference questions require you to understand why the author, narrator, or character mentions something. This usually has a lot to do with the type of passage you're dealing with:

- For **Expository Passages**, the reference will probably be used to describe or characterize something in the passage.
- For **Narrative Passages**, the reference will probably be used to provide details about the plot, characters, or other narrative elements.
- For **Persuasive Passages**, the reference will probably be used to strengthen the author's argument or weaken his opponent's position.

Whenever you're dealing with these types of questions, be sure to ask yourself, "What purpose does the reference serve in the context of the passage?"

Practice on the following passage.

The following passage considers the impact of a country's political and cultural history on methods of expression.

The term "political unconscious" refers to those things that are so ingrained in our culture that we do not consider them political or cultural, although they are. Because we, as members of a culture, work
5   within the confines of our "political unconscious," any narrative we may produce will be produced in accordance with our culture's "master narrative." The underlying implications of this idea provide a theoretical backdrop for the more specific theories of
10 gender and race. Thus there is an underlying cultural force that molds our discourse and our literature. Culture supplants nature in the formation of literature and discourse, and in the consequent formation of our cultural and personal identities.
15   The only effective liberation from such constraints begins with the recognition that there is nothing that is not social and historical – indeed, that everything is political. Thus, what constrains us is the fallacy that our basic assumptions are not a
20 product of our culture and our membership in it, but are in some way naturally generated. Everything is political because it is culturally rather than naturally constructed, and our interpretation of literature and discourse functions within the confines of these
25 constructs and must be read as such. Not only must we interpret the literature of a culture from a "political perspective," but also we must see all literature as a reflection of the culture's "master narrative."
30   In her essay, "Playing in the Dark," Toni Morrison[1] argues that the black presence in America is a defining feature of American literature and identity, though it has not previously been acknowledged as such. The "Africanist presence," as
35 Morrison calls it, is vital to the formation of the identity, and thus the literature, that is specific to America. She writes, "The concept of freedom did not emerge in a vacuum. Nothing highlighted freedom – if it did not in fact create it – like slavery."
40 The American dream of freedom and ownership, of democracy could not have been established without the visible presence of the lack of freedom, ownership, and democracy, which the slaves provided. This dream shaped the identity of the
45 white American. Thus, for Morrison, the creation of America's "master narrative" is dependent on what is superficially excluded from it. Morrison definitively states that: "The very manner by which American literature distinguishes itself as a coherent entity

50 exists because of this unsettled and unsettling population." In other words, the presence of black slaves and their freed descendants is what makes the American canon uniquely American.
      These theories are particularly useful in the
55 analysis and understanding of our culture's literature within a cultural context. In her work as a literary theorist and writer, Morrison turns an analytical eye on her constraints as a writer within the highly categorized world in which we live. Beyond the
60 context of literary analysis, Morrison calls attention to the fact that our culture is dominated by these culturally constructed groups and categories. The result of this, however, is somewhat paradoxical. Though they give us the tools to rethink and reform
65 the very way in which we perceive our own identities, they also reveal the great extent to which our culture has the power to define and confine us.

9

The "underlying cultural force" (line 10-11) can best be characterized as

A) a subtle influence
B) an overpowering imperative
C) a mysterious phenomenon
D) an insidious impediment

12

The "liberation" in line 15 is best understood as the

A) freedom from an oppressive convention
B) distinction between writing from different cultures
C) ignorance of effect of political influence on culture
D) ability to write in a culturally absolute sense

15

To Morrison, a "categorized world" (line 59) serves as

A) a function of an undeniable history
B) an obstacle to overcome
C) a useful result of intentional decisions
D) an unfortunate conceptualization

---

[1] Toni Morrison (1931-) is an American novelist, editor, and professor.

The Author Would Most Likely

The author would most likely describe the "happier state" (line 9) as a...

The author would most likely characterize the views of the "thinkers" referred to in line 28 as

These questions can feel quite difficult. You don't know the author, right? How the heck are you supposed to know what he's thinking?!?

The good news is that the passage **always** gives you enough information to know where the author stands on any particular issue. It's your job to find it.

Remember

✓ You are not expected to read between the lines.
✓ You should answer in your own words whenever possible.
✓ If you can't find support for an answer, it's not the correct answer.
✓ Use the **main purpose** or **main idea** of the passage to know where the author stands.

If you understand **why** the author wrote the passage, you'll be much more likely to know how he would address the issue.

For a **Narrative** passage, the author will generally only have an opinion if he's the narrator. What does he think of the events in the passage?

For a **Persuasive** passage, the author will probably believe something in line with his primary argument.

For an **Expository** passage, the author will probably believe in something that will aid in his characterization of the topic of the passage.

SAT READING
PASSAGE BASED QUESTIONS

…Mrs. Hudson, the landlady of my friend, was a long-suffering woman. Not only was her first-floor flat invaded at all hours by throngs of singular and often undesirable characters but her remarkable lodger showed an eccentricity and irregularity in his life which must have sorely tried her patience. His incredible untidiness, his addiction to music at strange hours, his occasional revolver practice within doors, his weird and often malodorous scientific experiments, and the atmosphere of violence and danger which hung around him made him the very worst tenant in London. On the other hand, his payments were princely. I have no doubt that the house might have been purchased at the price which Holmes paid for his rooms during the years that I was with him…

17

The author would most likely agree with which of the following statements?

A) Mrs. Hudson should probably evict Holmes.
B) Mrs. Hudson's ire is likely tempered by financial incentives.
C) Holmes is a disagreeable roommate.
D) Holmes's apartment is an inappropriate location for experimenting.

There is a particular spot within the National Statuary Hall in the United States Capitol that has a somewhat apocryphal history. Known as the "Whisper Spot," the location possesses interesting acoustical properties. The amphitheater dome allows a person standing on a specific floor tile to clearly hear a conversation from the other side of the hall – nearly 200 feet away.

It has been said that John Adams took advantage of the Hall's acoustics to surreptitiously eavesdrop on other politicians under the impression their words were secret. Today, one can stand near the floor plaque marking Adam's desk on the West side of the Hall while the other party stands at the corresponding spot on the East side. According to Capitol historian William C. Allen, the story began long after Adams' death as a tourism gimmick. While there is no documentation of a "Whisper Spot" prior to the early twentieth century, this fact alone does not discount its possible use for political reconnaissance.

10

The author would most likely agree with which of the following statements?

A) Lack of evidence proves very little.
B) Politicians are generally dishonest people.
C) Historians are the final authority on many matters.
D) The "Whisper Spot" has a history that is unlikely to be unraveled.

Down to Two Answer Choices?

This is going to happen a lot. You have followed the technique and eliminated three of the five Answer Choices. The remaining two Answer Choices both feel ok; you can't decide which one is correct. This is one reason most students don't like the Passage-Based questions.

Fear not – there is only one defensible correct answer. There is always something wrong with four of the five answer choices. Focus on finding the **wrong** answer choice, not the right one.

Examples of Wrong Answer Choices

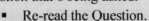

- ✕ Answer Choice doesn't answer the question being asked
  - ○ This is tricky; there is textual support for the Answer Choice, but, unfortunately, the Answer Choice doesn't answer the question that's being asked.
    - ▪ Re-read the Question.
- ✕ Answer Choice is half right
  - ○ This gets a lot of students, too. The first half of the Answer Choice is great, but there's something wrong with the second half.
    - ▪ The entire Answer Choice must be correct. If it makes a wrong turn at the end, get rid of it.
- ✕ Answer Choice goes beyond the text
  - ○ This can happen when you know a lot about the topic of the passage. If an Answer Choice isn't directly supported by the passage (even if it's true), you have to get rid of it.
    - ▪ Use the **point test**. If you can't point to the part of the passage that supports the Answer Choice, get rid of it.

If you're still not able to identify the correct answer after working through these categories, chances are you don't understand the passage, question, or Answer Choice(s). At this point, it's a good idea to skip the question.

Turn to this page whenever you're struggling to get down to one Answer Choice.

Tough Passages

Most students will find at least one or two difficult passages on the SAT. However, difficulty is a subjective property when it comes to Critical Reading, so we'll cover a few characteristics that make certain passages difficult for students.

> **Difficult Passage #1**
>
> The topic of the passage is BOOOORING.

> **Difficult Passage #2**
>
> The passage is full of difficult vocabulary words.

> **Difficult Passage #3**
>
> The author's argument or purpose is *arcane*, *abstruse*, or subtle.

> **Difficult Passage #4**
>
> The passage is supposed to be funny, but you don't get the humor.

> **Difficult Passage #5**
>
> The passage is so long that by the time you have finished, you forgot how it started.

Do any of these feel familiar? They should.

Now here's the good news: you can actively improve your critical reading skills by making use of the five following strategies.

 arcane: adj., known or understood by very few; mysterious; secret; obscure; esoteric

 abstruse: adj., hard to understand; recondite; esoteric

Problem	Solution
You find the passage tedious and boring.	SO WHAT?! You do boring things all the time. That doesn't mean you can't do them well. Pretend you're interested, and the time will go by much more quickly. If you force yourself to stay engaged, you'll get through the passage much more quickly and efficiently.
The passage is full of difficult vocabulary words.	If you don't know them now, you're definitely not going to know them for the test without putting in some serious work. Study the Hit List and any words you don't know in the practice passages. The good news is that having a stronger vocabulary will help on the entire Critical Reading section. You just might do a little better in school, too. Win-win.
The author's argument is difficult to understand.	Understanding persuasive language is helpful here. There are quite a few different means by which an author can get his point across. Study the chapter on rhetoric for a primer on different rhetorical devices. You should also highlight the areas of the passage that you did understand. Doing so may help you make a connection between the points and figure out the argument via deduction.
You don't get the joke.	You probably won't recognize this one, and that's usually not too much of a problem. However, the test WILL ask you about tone if you're dealing with a humorous passage, so if you get to a tone question and you don't detect a tone, go with something that means humorous.
The passages are extremely long.	The first thing you should do on a long passage is mentally prepare yourself. If you tell yourself not to panic and don't expect to get through the whole thing quickly, it will feel less intimidating Second, you should take notes next to each paragraph as you're reading the passage. One-sentence summaries will provide you will useful anchor points. Since the order of the questions generally follows the order of the passage, use these anchors to help yourself find support for your answers.

The following passage considers the impact of a country's political and cultural history on methods of expression.

The term "political unconscious" refers to those things that are so ingrained in our culture that we do not consider them political or cultural, although they are. Because we, as members of a culture, work within the confines of our "political unconscious," any narrative we may produce will be produced in accordance with our culture's "master narrative." The underlying implications of this idea provide a theoretical backdrop for the more specific theories of gender and race. Thus there is an underlying cultural force that molds our discourse and our literature. Culture supplants nature in the formation of literature and discourse, and in the consequent formation of our cultural and personal identities.

The only effective liberation from such constraints begins with the recognition that there is nothing that is not social and historical – indeed, that everything is political. Thus, what constrains us is the fallacy that our basic assumptions are not a product of our culture and our membership in it, but are in some way naturally generated. Everything is political because it is culturally rather than naturally constructed, and our interpretation of literature and discourse functions within the confines of these constructs and must be read as such. Not only must we interpret the literature of a culture from a "political perspective," but also we must see all literature as a reflection of the culture's "master narrative."

In her essay, "Playing in the Dark," Toni Morrison[1] argues that the black presence in America is a defining feature of American literature and identity, though it has not previously been acknowledged as such. The "Africanist presence," as Morrison calls it, is vital to the formation of the identity, and thus the literature, that is specific to America. She writes, "The concept of freedom did not emerge in a vacuum. Nothing highlighted freedom – if it did not in fact create it – like slavery." The American dream of freedom and ownership, of democracy could not have been established without the visible presence of the lack of freedom, ownership, and democracy, which the slaves provided. This dream shaped the identity of the white American. Thus, for Morrison, the creation of America's "master narrative" is dependent on what is superficially excluded from it. Morrison definitively states that: "The very manner by which American literature distinguishes itself as a coherent entity

exists because of this unsettled and unsettling population." In other words, the presence of black slaves and their freed descendants is what makes the American canon uniquely American.

These theories are particularly useful in the analysis and understanding of our culture's literature within a cultural context. In her work as a literary theorist and writer, Morrison turns an analytical eye on her constraints as a writer within the highly categorized world in which we live. Beyond the context of literary analysis, Morrison calls attention to the fact that our culture is dominated by these culturally constructed groups and categories. The result of this, however, is somewhat paradoxical. Though they give us the tools to rethink and reform the very way in which we perceive our own identities, they also reveal the great extent to which our culture has the power to define and confine us.

Writing paragraph summaries is a great way to make tough passages easier to understand and will force to you stick to questions you're more likely to get correct.

Paragraph 1: _____
_____
_____
_____

Paragraph 2: _____
_____
_____
_____

Paragraph 3: _____
_____
_____
_____

Paragraph 4: _____
_____
_____
_____

What is the main idea of this passage?
_____
_____
_____
_____

What type of passage is this?
_____

[1] Toni Morrison (born 1931) is an American novelist, editor, and professor.

No Line Reference

95% of the Critical Reading questions on the SAT provide a line or paragraph reference. When a question doesn't provide a line reference, your ability to find text quickly is what's being tested.

Examples of Questions without Line References

✓ "Both passages call attention to which aspect of <the topic>?"
✓ "The author of Passage 2 would most likely criticize the author of Passage 1 for…"
✓ "Which statement best describes the relationship between Passage 1 and Passage 2?"
✓ "The narrator mentions all of the following as problems EXCEPT…"

Luckily, the order of the questions generally follows the order of the passage. Where do you think you'll find the answer to number 12 in the examples below? _____

There are a distressing number of traditions observed in the United States that have become obsolete and thus deserve honest reevaluation. Many of these traditions have their origins in agrarian
5 considerations that are no longer significant. The country's continued observation of these archaic traditions speaks volumes about its reluctance to improve efficiency. Perhaps policy makers should consider the costs invoked by blind devotion to
10 policies that have outlived their usefulness.
Consider voting. In 1792, federal law chose November as a desirable month for elections because the harvest would have been completed and winter storms would not have begun. Tuesday was chosen
15 as the best day of the week because farmers needed a full day to travel by horse-drawn vehicle to the county seat to vote. "Why not Wednesday?", you might ask. Well, the legislators also wanted to avoid interfering with the Biblical Sabbath or with many
20 towns' market day. Such considerations are clearly out touch with the modern world.
The world has changed a lot since then, and many critics of the current electoral system rightly point out that holding elections on Tuesday makes voting much
25 more difficult for the majority of people who work a traditional Monday through Friday, 9am-5pm schedule. Granted, many employers provide an hour or two of paid leave to participate in elections…

11

As used in line 1, "observed" most nearly means

A) seen
B) practiced
C) remarked
D) opened

12

According to the author, the reasons for the current voting schedule can best be described as

A) anachronistic
B) laughable
C) legitimate
D) overbearing

13

In line 22, the author uses the phrase "the world has changed" to emphasize the

A) length of time since laws were last rejected
B) consternation with which he perceives the change
C) exasperation at a contemporary scenario
D) unusual state of affairs at the time of the laws' formation

Reading Approach – Hardcore Edition

OK, so you have mastered the individual steps of the approach and are starting to feel pretty good about it, but you're still making mistakes? Chances are high that you're not executing correctly on one of the steps of the approach.

The flow chart on the next page should be a handy reference. Just follow the steps exactly as written. No timer, no looking at the clock. Use the flow chart on every single question. You will do your absolute best. If you're still getting questions wrong, it's because your vocabulary or reading comprehension skills aren't as strong as they need to be. Practice reading and study vocabulary to get better.

Once your performance improves, begin working through the passages with a timer; you'll see that having a strong technique actually allows you to complete *more* of the test.

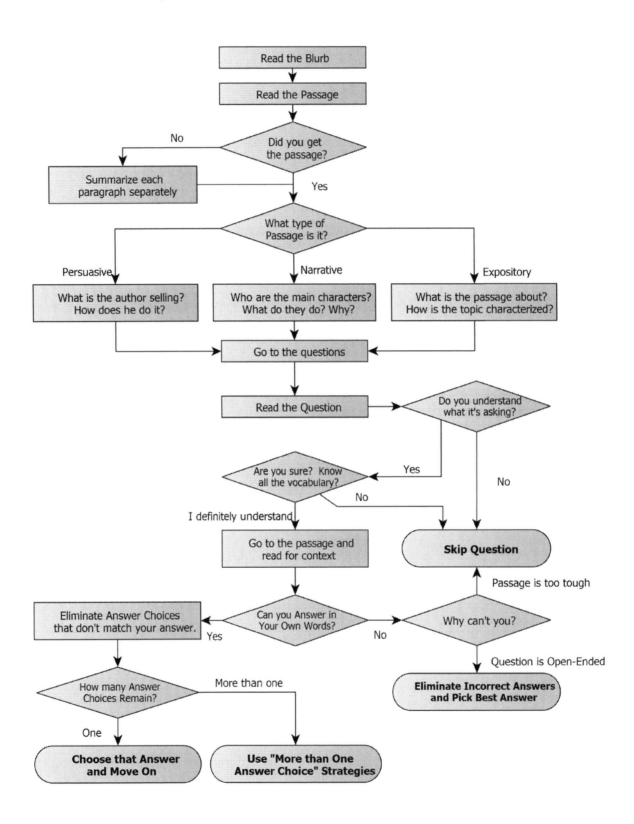

196

The Writing and Language Approach

On the Writing and Language test, you're going to be assessed on four dimensions:

1. **Rules of Written English Grammar:** The SAT tests a consistent, predictable set of grammar rules. Learn them and these questions are a breeze.
2. **Good Writing vs. Bad Writing:** Wordiness, redundancy, passive voice. These are all writing characteristics that aren't grammatically incorrect per se, but should be avoided.
3. **Understanding Context and Flow:** Good writing has a natural flow in which the conceptual links between sentences are clear and predictable. Transition words, conjunctions, and the order of sentences all play a big role here.
4. **Reading Comprehension:** Several questions may appear to have wandered onto this test from the prior test. Treat them like Reading questions (i.e., answer them in your own words) and you'll be fine.

The Approach

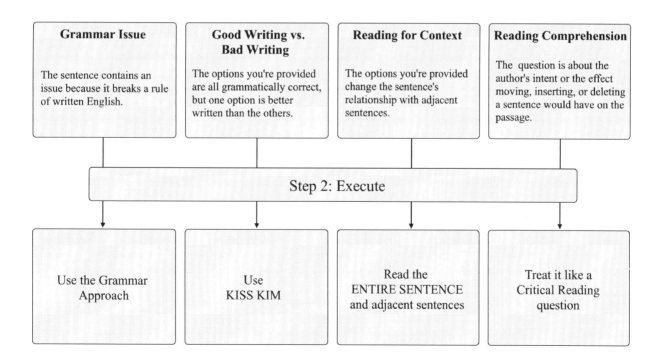

Step 1: Determine the Question Type

Grammar Issue	**Good Writing vs. Bad Writing**	**Reading for Context**	**Reading Comprehension**
The sentence contains an issue because it breaks a rule of written English.	The options you're provided are all grammatically correct, but one option is better written than the others.	The options you're provided change the sentence's relationship with adjacent sentences.	The question is about the author's intent or the effect moving, inserting, or deleting a sentence would have on the passage.

Step 2: Execute

Use the Grammar Approach	Use KISS KIM	Read the ENTIRE SENTENCE and adjacent sentences	Treat it like a Critical Reading question

Grammar Introduction

Grammar concepts will be tested on over 40% of the Writing and Language questions.

It's good to learn the rules. The following list is sorted by frequency: the higher an item is on the list, the more frequently you'll be tested on it.

The following list of rules is exhaustive; if a grammar rules isn't on the list, it's not tested on the SAT.

You're welcome.

Punctuation

✓ Semicolons are used to separate two independent clauses.

✓ Colons must be preceded by an independent clause and generally introduce a list or clarification.

✓ Dashes are used to set apart a descriptive phrase.

✓ Apostrophes are generally used to make nouns possessive or to form contractions; they're never used to make words plural.

Incorrect

It's hard to believe I could respect someone so much; going so far as to volunteer in his reelection campaign.

The keys to any successful party are: plenty of food and drinks, fun activities, and someone who is willing to put a lampshade on his head.

The city council member – the very same member who would later be implicated in an embarrassing scandal, was a vocal crusader for ethics in politics.

Its imperative that any country must consider the potential outcomes of it's military interventions.

Correct

It's hard to believe I could respect someone so much; I went as far as volunteering in his reelection campaign.

These are the keys to any successful party: plenty of food and drinks, fun activities, and someone who is willing to put a lampshade on his head.

The city council member – the very same member who would later be implicated in an embarrassing scandal – was a vocal crusader for ethics in politics.

It's imperative that any country must consider the potential outcomes of its military interventions.

Comma Usage

- ✓ Commas are generally used to add a pause in a sentence.

- ✓ Commas can replace the word "and" between two **similar** adjectives or adverbs.

- ✓ A *comma splice* is an error that occurs when two independent clauses are joined with only a comma.

- ✓ Commas (or long dashes) can also be used to set off an *appositive*, which is a short descriptive clause that is not essential to the structure of the sentence.

Incorrect

The judge's nomination came as a surprise to us all, his conservative views were seen as troubling, even divisive.

The collapsible versatile workbench which I bought for a great price from my neighbor fell apart surprisingly quickly so I asked for a refund.

Correct

The judge's nomination came as a surprise to us all; his conservative views were seen as troubling, even divisive.

The collapsible, versatile workbench, which I bought for a great price from my neighbor, fell apart surprisingly quickly, so I asked for a refund.

Pronoun Agreement

- ✓ A pronoun must always agree in number with its antecedent.

Incorrect

The university took great pride in their rigorous Ultimate Frisbee tournament.

Each of the plotlines of the intricate fantasy book could attract a different group of followers because they offer compelling themes.

Correct

The university took great pride in its rigorous Ultimate Frisbee tournament.

Each of the plotlines of the intricate fantasy book could attract a different group of followers because it offers compelling themes.

Verb Tense

✓ Verb tense (e.g., past, future, etc.) must match the time period of the sentence and be consistent with or complementary to the rest of the sentence. The verb also needs to have a legitimate verb formation.

Incorrect

In 1879, Nikola Tesla will file the first radio patent, at least a decade before Guglielmo Marconi – the man generally credited with the feat – filed a patent of his own.

The champion has swam across the English Channel four times; I would of done the same had it not been for my crippling lack of cardiovascular fitness.

Correct

In 1879, Nikola Tesla filed the first radio patent, at least a decade before Guglielmo Marconi – the man generally credited with the feat – filed a patent of his own.

The champion has swum across the English Channel four times; I would have done the same had it not been for my crippling lack of cardiovascular fitness.

Parallelism

✓ Lists and parallel structures (such as comparisons and idiomatic constructions) must maintain the same format.

Incorrect

It's much easier to master Guitar Hero than becoming truly proficient with a six-string guitar.

In response to the environmental disaster, the volunteer group picketed corporate headquarters, started a letter-writing campaign, and were asking people to donate to the cause.

Correct

It's much easier to master Guitar Hero than to become truly proficient with a six-string guitar.

In response to the environmental disaster, the volunteer group picketed corporate headquarters, started a letter-writing campaign, and asked people to donate to the cause.

Preposition Usage

  ✓ Certain words (generally verbs, nouns, and adjectives) require specific prepositions.

Incorrect

Our team has worked for several months on a robot that we plan on submitting to the robotics division of the science fair.

Andy was ordered to visit a nutritionist in conjunction to his regular doctor.

Correct

Our team has worked for several months on a robot that we plan to submit to the robotics division of the science fair.

Andy was ordered to visit a nutritionist in conjunction with his regular doctor.

Subject-Verb Agreement

  ✓ The subject and corresponding verb must agree in number.

Incorrect

The most important factor to consider when looking at used cars are whether the previous owners were diligent with maintenance work.

Each of the competitors are worthy of the grand prize, but only one can win.

Correct

The most important factor to consider when looking at used cars is whether the previous owners were diligent with maintenance work.

Each of the competitors is worthy of the grand prize, but only one can win.

Homophones

✓ Homophones are words that sound alike but have different meanings. It's important not to mix them up.

Incorrect

For my research paper, I sighted the online social media sight's newsfeed, but my teacher told me cite unseen that I would need better sources.

Chantel would rather dispassionately discuss the effects of the policy proposal then get involved in an emotional argument regarding it's ethics.

Correct

For my research paper, I cited the online social media site's newsfeed, but my teacher told me sight unseen that I would need better sources.

Chantel would rather dispassionately discuss the effects of the policy proposal than get involved in an emotional argument regarding its ethics.

Sentence Fragment

✓ A sentence must be a complete thought that can stand on its own.

Incorrect

Since I switched to a Raw Foods diet, which emphasizes regular consumption of unprocessed, natural foods over many commonly available packaged food products.

The film, an overly complex and ultimately unsatisfying attempt at meta art, managing to obscure tremendous talent with overwrought, forced writing.

Correct

I switched to a Raw Foods diet, which emphasizes regular consumption of unprocessed, natural foods over many commonly available packaged food products.

The film, an overly complex and ultimately unsatisfying attempt at meta art, manages to obscure tremendous talent with overwrought, forced writing.

Misplaced Modifier

✓ Descriptive phrases must be adjacent to whatever they're describing.

Incorrect

After spending four years working diligently, Tom's diploma hung proudly in his office.

Staring out the window, Ryan's problems didn't seem so insurmountable.

Correct

After spending four years working diligently, Tom hung his diploma proudly in his office.

When Ryan stared out the window, his problems didn't seem so insurmountable.

Idiomatic Usage

✓ The English language requires certain consistent constructions
(e.g., "not only…but also, as…as, etc.).

Incorrect

Not only did the committee miss the point of my Reusable Bathroom Tissue ad campaign, and they accused me of being a threat to public health.

Twice as many government officials opposed the new piece of legislation than supported it.

Correct

Not only did the committee miss the point of my Reusable Bathroom Tissue ad campaign, but they accused me of being a threat to public health.

Twice as many government officials opposed the new piece of legislation as supported it.

Pronoun Case

✓ A pronoun can either be a subject (e.g., I, he, she, we, they) or an object (e.g., me, him, her, us, them). The case must match the pronoun's role in the sentence.

Incorrect

The teacher told Bobby and I to stop passing notes during class or risk having them read aloud.

He did a way better job than me.

Correct

The teacher told Bobby and me to stop passing notes during class or risk having them read aloud.

He did a way better job than I.

Pronoun Ambiguity

✓ The relationship between a pronoun and its antecedent must be clear and explicit.

Incorrect

Tom, Sara, and Jamie all went to the mall together, but he couldn't take the crowds and had to leave early.

Nicole had a present for Gina, but couldn't deliver it because she was busy at work.

Correct

Tom, Sara, and Jamie all went to the mall together, but Jamie couldn't take the crowds and had to leave early.

Nicole had a present for Gina, but couldn't deliver it because Gina was busy at work.

Noun Agreement

✓ When appropriate, corresponding nouns must agree in number.

Incorrect

The stranded survivors decided to make their last stand against the zombie invasion, grabbed their weapon, and charged into battle, only to be eaten alive.

Anyone considering a career in engineering must be skilled mathematicians and communicators.

Correct

The stranded survivors decided to make their last stand against the zombie invasion, grabbed their weapons, and charged into battle, only to be eaten alive.

Anyone considering a career in engineering must be a skilled mathematician and communicator.

Punctuation

Punctuation is tested all over the SAT. Here's what you need to know.

Semicolons

Ah, the humble semicolon. Though you may not know what it's called, you have no doubt seen it. As it's tested on the SAT, the semicolon is basically a weak period. Be sure that you have an independent clause on both sides of the semicolon. Simple.

- ✓ independent cause ; independent clause

- ✗ dependent cause ; dependent clause

- ✗ dependent cause ; independent clause

- ✗ independent clause ; dependent clause

Semicolons can also be used to fix a comma splice. Just transform the comma into a semicolon and you're in business.

Incorrect

Something about the teacher's admonition must have motivated the students; finishing the project a full three days before it was due.

On hot days, a pig will cover itself with mud to cool down because it can't perspire, this contradicts the validity of the common phrase "I'm sweating like a pig."

Correct

Something about the teacher's admonition must have motivated the students; we finished the project a full three days before it was due.

On hot days, a pig will cover itself with mud to cool down because it can't perspire; this contradicts the validity of the common phrase "I'm sweating like a pig."

5 Born out of the necessity for cheap and edible crops for the poor. The dish was most commonly referred to as "cottage pie".

5

A) NO CHANGE
B) The dish most commonly referred to as "cottage pie" was a necessity for cheap and edible crops for the poor.
C) Cottage pie was born out of the necessity for cheap and edible crops for the poor.
D) Born of out necessity for cheap and edible crops for the poor; The dish was most referred to as "cottage pie."

17 Owls awaken at night, the parents go out to hunt for food.

17

A) NO CHANGE
B) Owls awaken at night, then the parents go out to hunt for food.
C) Owls awaken at night, and the parents go out to hunt for food.
D) Owls awaken at night: the parents go out to hunt for food.

Colons

Colons are generally used to introduce a list or clarifying phrase. The important thing to remember with colons is that you need an independent clause *before* the colon. After the colon, anything goes.

Incorrect

Before takeoff, the plane's crew went through the pre-flight checklist, including: verifying fuel levels, visually inspecting all windows and doors, and running a systems check.

Correct

Before takeoff, the plane's crew went through the pre-flight checklist: verifying fuel levels, visually inspecting all windows and doors, and running a systems check.

Before takeoff, the plane's crew went through the pre-flight checklist, including verifying fuel levels, visually inspecting all windows and doors, and running a systems check.

8 To ensure the proper address, send the money to: 555 Main Street, Columbus, GA, 22234.

8
A) NO CHANGE
B) Make sure to send the money to the proper address:
C) Make sure to send the money to the proper address to,
D) Make sure to send the money to the proper address;

The following teams have absolutely no **10** chance of making the playoffs: The Hornets, The Pelicans, The Magic, and The Wizards.

10
A) NO CHANGE
B) chance of making the playoffs;
C) chance of making the playoffs,
D) chance to make the playoffs:

Long Dashes

Long dashes can be used like commas – for example, to set aside a string of descriptive language know as an appositive – or like colons – to introduce a list or clarification. They're basically the Swiss army punctuation.

Incorrect

The deep-sea diver–who had twenty years of experience, was sure to take the proper precautions before entering the water.

The four year old received a bevy of gifts under the tree, dolls, games, dresses, even candy.

Correct

The deep-sea diver – who had twenty years of experience – was sure to take the proper precautions before entering the water.

The four year old received a bevy of gifts under the tree – dolls, games, dresses, even candy.

---

8 Arundhati Roy, an Indian author – is best known for her novel *The God of Small Things*, which won the Man Booker Prize for Fiction in 1997.

8

A) NO CHANGE
B) Arundhati Roy, an Indian author who is best known for her novel
C) Arundhati Roy – an Indian author – is best known for her novel
D) Arundhati Roy is an Indian author, she is best known for her novel

---

Generally speaking, there are three categories into which all things can be placed, animal, vegetable, and mineral.

10

A) NO CHANGE
B) placed – animal, vegetable, and mineral.
C) placed; animal, vegetable, and mineral.
D) placed, such as :animal, vegetable, and mineral.

Apostrophes

Apostrophes are used to transform a word into a possessive and to form contractions. Pretty simple. Unfortunately, conflicts can occur when there's overlap or you have contractions that sound like each other.

A good way to tell whether it's appropriate to use an apostrophe is to expand the word and see if it still works in the sentence.

Incorrect

My parents told me I'm no longer covered by they're medical insurance.

If I had known you were coming, I would of baked a cake.

Correct

My parents told me I'm no longer covered by their medical insurance.

If I had known you were coming, I would've baked a cake.

It was one of the worst days of my life when my **15** guitars neck split into two pieces. Alas, I had rocked just a little too hard.

15
A) NO CHANGE
B) guitars' neck
C) guitar's neck
D) guitar neck

Despite the **21** childrens' protests, the popular entertainer refused to sing Happy Birthday due to a cease-and-desist letter from the song's copyright holder.

21
A) NO CHANGE
B) childrens
C) children's
D) childrens's

Before we left **8** for vacation; we made sure that all of our bags were packed.

8

A) NO EROR
B) for vacation we made sure that
C) for vacation, we made sure that
D) for vacation: we made sure that

When the GameCube was on the brink of failure, Capcom devised a marketing strategy to help breathe life into the dying system. They created a series of games called **10** the Capcom Five, *P.N.03, Viewtiful Joe, Dead Phoenix, Resident Evil 4, and Killer7.*

10

A) NO ERROR
B) the Capcom Five.
C) the Capcom Five;
D) the Capcom Five:

Her brand new puppy was adorable and **12** curious, he burrowed himself under the couch cushions and took a quick nap.

12

A) NO ERROR
B) curious, and so he burrowed himself
C) curious. Because he burrowed himself
D) curious: he burrowed himself

Superstorm **14** Sandy, the deadliest and most destructive hurricane of the 2012 Atlantic hurricane season – was the second-costliest hurricane in United States history.

14

A) NO ERROR
B) Sandy the
C) Sandy – the
D) Sandy; the

Comma Usage

Commas can be used in a whole bunch of different applications. The SAT tests most of them.

Separating Clauses

A comma splice is an error that occurs when you join two independent clauses (strings of words that could stand on their own as a complete sentence) with only a comma.

Incorrect

I drove my girlfriend to Denny's for our anniversary, that's when I became single.

There are two ways to fix a comma splice:

---

1. Make one of the independent clauses into a dependent clause.

*I drove my girlfriend to Denny's for our anniversary, **and** that's when I became single.*

***When** I drove my girlfriend to Denny's for our anniversary, ~~that's when~~ I became single.*

---

2. Use a semicolon or period instead of a comma.

I drove my girlfriend to Denny's for our anniversary; that's when I became single.

I drove my girlfriend to Denny's for our anniversary. That's when I became single.

Creating Appositives

An appositive clause is technically a noun or phrase that renames or describes another noun right beside it. Like this:

The big dog, brown and full of life, was allowed to roam freely throughout the house.

The phrase "brown and full of life" is an appositive clause. It is adding description to the dog, but it's not actually necessary to the sentence. You can easily check this by removing the prhase from the sentence. If it still makes sense, the phrase was an appositve.

The big brown dog was allowed to roam freely throughout the house.

See?

We create and offset appositive clauses by surrounding them by either commas or dashes.

Incorrect

The distinguished director, who was known as a bit of an iconoclast was late to his own premier.

During lunch Joanna the messiest eater since the dawn of time, left a wake of destruction throughout the dining room.

Correct

The distinguished director, who was known as a bit of an iconoclast, was late to his own premier.

During lunch, Joanna, the messiest eater since the dawn of time, left a wake of destruction throughout the dining room.

Ancient Norse literature is rich with folklore and popular beliefs, many **8** elements of it have counterparts in modern legends.

A) NO CHANGE
B) elements of which have counterparts in
C) elements that have counterparts for
D) of its elements have counterparts with

28 Vicki had never seen anything like this style of painting before, Vicki thought she was looking at photographs, not paint and canvas.

A) NO CHANGE
B) Vicki never saw
C) Never had Vicki seen
D) Never having seen

Contrary to what many people believe, searing meat does not seal in the moisture. **23** It is however essential to creating a brown crust with a rich flavor that is highly desirable.

A) NO CHANGE
B) It is, however
C) It is, however,
D) It, is however,

As a composer, John **2** Williams has enriched the world of cinema music, he uses as his work's inspiration elements of the movies' themes.

A) NO CHANGE
B) Williams has enriched the world of cinema music with works inspired by
C) Williams, who has enriched the world of cinema music by works whose inspirations are
D) Williams, enriching the world of cinema music, with works inspired by

Foxes must leave the safety of the den to hunt for food many times a **5** day, they are risking being eaten by predators or hunted by humans.

A) NO CHANGE
B) day at the risk of being eaten
C) day risking them to be eaten
D) day; the risk is to be eaten

Pronoun Agreement

Pronouns need to agree in number with the nouns or other pronouns (a.k.a. antecedents) they replace.

This is sometimes simple:

*Richard told me **he** was tired of people making fun of **his** nickname.*

*In order to appeal to a wide audience, television stations have to sequence shows in such a way that **viewers** do not have to wait too long before seeing a show **they** like.*

It can get more complicated when you're dealing with words that *might* be plural.

*Famous for **their** sticky feet, the **gecko** can run up walls and across ceilings as well as hang from a surface by **its** toes.*

Which is correct – "their" or "its"?

The test can also switch pronouns mid-sentence.

*Although **its** reputation is not as good as it once was, the bank is still proud of **their** productive, intelligent employees, many of whom have served time in federal prison.*

 In each case, you must verify what specifically the pronoun is referring to and whether it should be singular or plural.

Singular	Plural
I	we
me	us
myself	ourselves
you	you
yourself	yourselves
he, she, it	they, them
his, her, hers, its	their, theirs
himself, herself, itself	themselves
him, her, it	them
who	who
which	which
that	that

If you want to learn to play guitar, a book can tell you how to form chords or strum properly, but **5** they cannot take the place of hands-on experience.

A) NO CHANGE
B) they however
C) it
D) those books

Even after the loss of several writers, the comedy troupe is still proud of **21** their recent endeavor, an undeniably mediocre film.

A) NO CHANGE
B) they're
C) it's
D) its

In order to attract a loyal customer base, **26** casinos have to display signs and train dealers in such a way that gamblers receive instructions that you can understand.

A) NO CHANGE
B) casinos have to display signs and train dealers in such a way that gamblers receive instructions that he or she understands
C) casinos have to display signs and train dealers in such a way that gamblers receive instructions that they can understand
D) in such a way that gamblers can understand instructions, casinos have to display signs and train dealers

Collective Nouns are particularly *pernicious*. They're **always** singular.

army	committee	faculty	majority	senate
audience	company	family	minority	society
board	corporation	firm	navy	team
cabinet	council	group	public	troupe
class	department	jury	school	

pernicious: adj, causing insidious harm or ruin; ruinous; injurious; hurtful

217

Verb Tense

Incorrect

In 1952, Jonas Salk will develop a vaccine for polio and distribute it freely in 1955.

Correct

In 1952, Jonas Salk developed a vaccine for polio and distributed it freely in 1955.

Simply put, Incorrect Verb Tense refers to an instance in which the verb doesn't match with the time period of the rest of the sentence or violates conjunction rules.

The wrong verb tense can be obvious to spot, or it can be very subtle. Here are the different ways in which it will manifest itself, from simplest to most difficult.

Alana was sitting on the living room couch, engrossed in her needlepoint, when the news report abruptly **16** recalling her to the present moment.

16

A) NO ERROR
B) would recall
C) will recall
D) recalled

A thick growth of bamboo shoots **20** standing thirty feet tall, their delicate reeds swayed gently in the breeze.

20

A) NO ERROR
B) standing thirty feet tall, their delicate reeds swaying
C) stood thirty feet tall, their delicate reeds swaying
D) stood thirty feet tall, and their delicate reeds swaying

That I now have little interest in religion is not the fault of my mother, **28** taking me to weekly meetings and conventions from the time I was two years old.

28

A) NO ERROR
B) who took
C) who has taken
D) who will take

As the price of gasoline rises and concern about the environmental effects of hydraulic fracturing **32** mounted, the natural gas industry is racing to create extraction methods not harmful to local ecosystems.

32

A) NO ERROR
B) will mount
C) mounts
D) had mounted

Parallelism

Parallelism is the requirement that all items in a list or part of a comparison all be in the same form. So, if you see a list or a comparison, check for proper parallelism. It's easier to spot if you know to look for it.

Incorrect

To pass the time, I enjoy reading, cycling, and to get destroyed on Call of Duty.

In movies, the best ways to destroy a vampire are to use a wooden stake or chopping its head off.

Correct

*To pass the time, I enjoy **reading**, **cycling**, and **getting** destroyed on Call of Duty.*

*In movies, the best ways to destroy a vampire are to **use** a wooden stake or **chop** its head off.*

My brother and I cherish memories of spending hours outdoors as children, climbing trees, building forts, throwing rocks at each other, and **4** the search for frogs.

4
A) NO ERROR
B) we would also search
C) to search
D) searching

During the meeting with Ryan's parent, the counselor mentioned that Ryan's application had demonstrated **6** considerable strength in extracurricular activities and to get a solid GPA.

6
A) NO ERROR
B) strength that was considerable in extracurricular activities as well as in getting
C) considerable strength in extracurricular activities and
D) considerable strength for extracurricular activities and

When I learned that both games were scheduled for the same evening, I found it difficult to choose between watching the basketball game **8** or to follow the soccer match.

8
A) NO ERROR
B) or following
C) and following
D) and to follow

Preposition Error

These are rare. Some verbs or nouns just require certain prepositions. Don't worry about memorizing all possible combinations. If you read a lot, you'll probably spot these errors when they (very infrequently) appear.

Incorrect

Stephen Hawking is regarded by many to be the foremost living authority on theoretical physics and may eventually help formulate a grand unifying theory.

After lunch, the group was planning on going to the movies.

Correct

Stephen Hawking is regarded by many as the foremost living authority on theoretical physics and may eventually help formulate a grand unifying theory.

After lunch, the group was planning to go to the movies.

---

3 Because practice tests require for one to complete each section without there having to be interruptions, it is a good idea to find a quiet spot where such disruptions are unlikely.

3

A) NO CHANGE
B) Because practice tests require that one complete each section without interruption,
C) Practice tests require that one complete each section without interruption and
D) When completing practice tests it is advisable for one to work without interruption and therefore

---

Today in class we discussed the logical, but mistaken, assumption that when politicians are no longer in public service they are incapable **5** to be well-connected lobbyists.

5

A) NO CHANGE
B) for being
C) of being
D) as being

A professor with years of in-classroom experience, Dr. Defusco was **7** regarded by many to be the world's foremost expert on the effects of dander on the environment.

7

A) NO CHANGE
B) regarded by many as
C) regarded to be by many
D) regarded by many as if he was

Subject-Verb Agreement Error

The subject and main verb must agree in number.

Incorrect

The student majoring in Liberal Arts study the exquisite Picasso collection between cooking batches of French fries.

Correct

The student majoring in Liberal Arts studies the exquisite Picasso collection between cooking batches of French fries.

Seems like a fairly simple concept, right? It is. There are four tricks the SAT uses to obscure what should be the easiest error to spot.

The subject and verb are separated by a long string of words.

The Yellow Warbler's songs, each more intricate and beautiful than the last, **1** is sung almost exclusively by the male birds.

1

A) NO CHANGE
B) are sung
C) have been sung
D) is sang

Each of the three movements of Radiohead's hit *Paranoid Android*, though totally different in structure and tempo, **3** blends with one another to form a cohesive whole.

3

A) NO CHANGE
B) blend
C) have blended
D) DELETE the underlined portion

The sentence tests conjunction rules.

Both his commitment to community outreach and his efforts to raise youth engagement **5** has gained Mr. Rogers the respect of the entire neighborhood.

5

A) NO CHANGE
B) have gained
C) had gained
D) will have gained

Despite their best efforts, neither my sisters nor my brother **7** knows the secret location of my prized cookie stash.

7

A) NO CHANGE
B) know
C) have known
D) would of known

The sentence uses collective nouns.

A series of guest lecturers on forensic sciences

9 are scheduled for this semester in Mr. Drexler's

biology class.

The United States Supreme Court, regarded as the

final authority on the Constitution, **11** and they

have recently wielded this power to uphold the

Affordable Care Act.

9
A) NO CHANGE
B) is scheduled
C) are on the schedule
D) will have been scheduled

11
A) NO CHANGE
B) and it ha
C) have
D) has

The sentence places the subject after the verb.

There **13** is many difficulties associated with

beginning a fitness regimen.

13
A) NO CHANGE
B) is many difficulties associating
C) are many difficulties associated
D) are many difficulties which associates

Standing beyond the velvet rope, to our amazement,

15 was Ryan and Dennis, both of whom had

supposedly disappeared earlier in the evening to head

back to the hotel.

15
A) NO CHANGE
B) is
C) were
D) have been

Subject-Verb Agreement Rules

For Conjunctions…

- …if two subjects are joined by an *and*, the verb must be plural.
- …if two subjects are joined by an *or* or *nor*, the verb must agree with the closer subject.

Collective Nouns (e.g., company, team, government, etc.) are always singular and thus need singular verbs.

Homophones

You probably learned about homophones in 3rd grade. You probably also forgot about that lesson almost immediately because, hey, who's going to mix these words up? Unfortunately, it tends to happen way more frequently than you'd think. Seriously. Check Facebook if you don't believe it.

Incorrect

I'd rather study hard for 12 years then spend the rest of my life making easily avoidable writing mistakes.

The site of Headless Horseman caused Ichabod Crane to head to the ancient burial sight to resight the spiritual incantation.

Correct

I'd rather study hard for 12 years than spend the rest of my life making easily avoidable writing mistakes.

The sight of Headless Horseman caused Ichabod Crane to head to the ancient burial site to recite the spiritual incantation.

Here is a list of homophones we have seen on past administrations of the SAT. Learn them.

Word	Definition
affect	to change or make a difference to
effect	a result; to bring about a result
accept	to agree to
except	not including
there	a location designation
they're	a contraction of "they are"
their	belonging to *them*
it's	a contraction of "it is"
its	belonging to *it*
then	taking place after something
than	a word used for comparisons
sight	the ability to see; vision
site	location of; internet location
cite	to attribute the source of
bare	naked; to uncover
bear	to carry; put up with
faze	momentarily stun
phase	state of matter; transition

The overuse of lens-flare was beginning to have the
3 opposite of the intended affect; rather than
lending a stylized and interesting element to the
shots, it was making them all look the same.

A) NO CHANGE
B) opposite of the intended affect,
C) opposite of the intended effect;
D) opposite of the intended effect,

The onslaught of enemies finally became too much
for **5** him to bear, so he unceremoniously quit the
match.

A) NO CHANGE
B) for bearing
C) him to bare,
D) his bearing

Even though going to the dentist was one of his least
favorite activities, **7** it was better then the
alternative: a lifetime of gingivitis.

A) NO CHANGE
B) it was better than the alternative:
C) it was better then the alternative;
D) it was alternatively better than

The child was **9** being lead around on a leash, as
though he was a puppy.

A) NO CHANGE
B) being lead on a leash
C) being leaded around on a leash
D) being led around on a leash

Sentence Fragment

A sentence fragment is a string of words that cannot stand on its own as a complete sentence.

You can turn a complete sentence into a fragment by adding or subtracting a word, usually a subordinating conjunction, such as since or after or conjunctions and pronouns such as which or that.

Incorrect

Several of the blockbuster movies that came out this summer which are popular because people are stupid.

Several of the blockbuster movies came out this summer are popular because people are stupid.

Correct

Several of the blockbuster movies that came out this summer are popular because people are stupid.

> **How to Identify Sentence Fragments**
>
> 1. First, take your pencil and cross out prepositional phrases, which add length to a sentence and obscure the main idea.
>
>> Several of the blockbuster movies ~~that came out this summer~~ are popular because people are stupid.
>
> 2. Second, watch out for relative pronouns and prepositions; they can be inserted into a sentence easily and ruin the whole thing.
>
>> Several of the blockbuster movies ~~that came out this summer~~ *which* are popular because people are stupid.

A complete sentence can become a sentence fragment really easily.

Complete	**Incomplete**
Donald Trump became the president.	*Since Donald Trump became president.*

Several of the house parties that occurred this weekend **4** which were because some parents were out of town.

A) NO CHANGE
B) because some parents were out of town
C) are because parents were out of town
D) happened from parents being out of town

Bill and Hillary Clinton's Global **13** Initiative was established to encourage global leaders to innovate solutions to pressing world issues, was created in 2005 and includes an annual convention for college students.

A) NO CHANGE
B) Initiative is established
C) Initiative, establishing
D) Initiative, established

22 *Mr. Robot,* a meandering and eerily dark work of fiction, primarily focused on the resurgence of the hacking community that has arisen in tandem with the explosion of social media in our current society.

A) NO CHANGE
B) *Mr Robot,* a meandering and eerily dark work of fiction, primarily focused on the resurgence of the hacking community that has arisen in tandem with the explosion of social media in our current society.
C) *Mr Robot* is primarily focused on the resurgence of the hacking community that has arisen in tandem with the explosion of social media in our current society. It is meandering and eerily dark as well.
D) A meandering and eerily dark work of fiction, *Mr. Robot* is primarily focused on the resurgence of the hacking community that has arisen in tandem with the explosion of social media in our current society.

27 Born out of the necessity for cheap and edible crops for the poor. The dish was most commonly referred to as "cottage pie".

A) NO CHANGE
B) The dish most commonly referred to as "cottage pie" was a necessity for cheap and edible crops for the poor.
C) Cottage pie was born out of the necessity for cheap and edible crops for the poor.
D) Born of out necessity for cheap and edible crops for the poor; The dish was most referred to as "cottage pie."

Misplaced Modifier

A misplaced modifier (also known as a dangling participle) is a descriptive phrase that isn't *adjacent* to what it's intended to describe or modify. There are two ways to fix misplaced modifiers.

1. Rearrange the sentence so the modifying phrase and what it's modifying are right next to each other.
2. Change the modifying phrase so it contains what is being modified.

Incorrect

While cleaning out the attic, my brother and I found a board game in a cabinet we used to play with.

While jogging down the street, my iPod began playing Backstreet Boys.

Correct

While cleaning out the attic, my brother and I found in a cabinet a board game **we used to play**.

While **I was** jogging down the street, my iPod began playing Backstreet Boys.

6 Not filling out the form punctually, there was a penalty fee in registering his class.

6
A) NO CHANGE
B) The form, not filled out punctually
C) Not punctually filling out the forms
D) Because he had not filled out the form punctually

8 Dressed in a sloppy, unkempt outfit, it reflected the lazy manner of the student as he strolled lazily into Anthropology class.

8
A) NO CHANGE
B) Dressed in a sloppy, unkempt outfit, the lazy manner of the student was reflected
C) Dressing a sloppy, unkempt outfit that reflected the lazy manner of the student
D) The sloppy, unkempt outfit of the student reflected his lazy manner

During my most recent college visit, I stumbled upon a wonderful sandwich shop **10** wandering in the adjacent town.

10
A) NO CHANGE
B) while I was wandering
C) while wandering
D) after wandering

Idiomatic Usage

On the SAT, we have to worry about **Correlative Conjunctions.**

both... and
either... or
neither... nor
not only... but also
whether... or

These are super important; you'll see at least two or three of these per test. These **always** come in pairs: if you start a phrase with one, you need to resolve with the other.

Unlike Jeff, **32** neither Billie or her younger sister Nina has an interest in a career in music.

32

A) NO CHANGE
B) not just Billie but
C) neither Billie nor
D) either Billie nor

The news media criticized the local government for failing either to repair the crumbling infrastructure **34** nor provide the necessary funding.

34

A) NO CHANGE
B) nor providing
C) or by providing
D) or to provide

Not only was the work he provided sloppy and **36** unfocused, and it was tardy.

36

A) NO CHANGE
B) unfocused, and also it was tardy.
C) unfocused; and it was tardy.
D) unfocused, but it was also tardy.

No sooner had he finished grading his final paper of the year **38** when a student showed up for office hours.

38

A) NO CHANGE
B) but a student showed up for office hours.
C) than a student showed up for office hours.
D) and a student showed up for office hours.

Pronoun Case Error

Some pronouns are subjects. Some pronouns are objects. Be sure to use them in the appropriate places.

Incorrect

Between you and I, the amount of attention that we as a nation give to celebrity gossip is troubling; this obsession prevents us from discussing more serious matters.

Correct

Between you and me, the amount of attention that we as a nation give to celebrity gossip is troubling; this obsession prevents us from discussing more serious matters.

Pronouns that are Subjects	Pronouns that are Objects	Possessive Pronouns
I	me	my (mine)
you	you	your (yours)
he, she, it	him, her, it	his, her (hers), it (its)
we	us	our (ours)
they	them	their (theirs)
who	whom	whose

My father always gave **13** my brother and I the same types of toys when we were younger so that neither of us would be envious of the other.

13

A) NO CHANGE
B) my brother and me
C) my brother and myself
D) both my brother and I

The police officer asked my friend and **15** I did either of us notice a suspicious package sitting in the corner of the park this morning.

15

A) NO CHANGE
B) I whether either of us noticed
C) me did either of us notice
D) me whether either of us had noticed

The results of the election reveal that one cannot reliably make inferences about people **17** whom vote for a particular candidate.

17

A) NO CHANGE
B) whom votes
C) who votes
D) who vote

Pronoun Ambiguity

Because pronouns can take the place of so many words, there is sometimes confusion in a sentence regarding exactly which noun is being replaced. That's called pronoun ambiguity. It's bad.

You can fix pronoun ambiguity errors by clarifying the specific relationship between the pronoun and the correct antecedent. Or you can just get rid of the pronoun and rewrite a bit.

Incorrect

Neither Namita nor Shannon believes that reading as many books as her son Josh does will lead to anything negative.

Unlike a tube amplifier, which works by using fragile vacuum tubes to amplify sounds, a solid state amp, which they often call an inferior product, works more consistently and requires less maintenance and care.

Correct

Neither Namita nor Shannon believes that reading as many books as Namita's son Josh does will lead to anything negative.

Unlike a tube amplifier, which works by using fragile vacuum tubes to amplify sounds, a solid state amp, which is often called an inferior product, works more consistently and requires less maintenance and care.

When Jackie and Jill visited the bar, **5** she noticed that the happy hour specials had changed and that their favorite drinks were no longer discounted.

5
A) NO CHANGE
B) she notices that the happy hour specials have changed
C) Jackie has noticed the happy hour specials changed
D) Jackie noticed that the happy hour specials had changed

"Who's on First" is generally regarded as one of the greatest comedy routines of all time. It was created by both William "Bud" Abbott and Lou Costello, **17** but he is usually cited as the more comedic of the duo. This is most likely due to the common belief that the "straight man" is the less funny man.

17

A) NO CHANGE
B) but he was the more comedic of the two.
C) but Costello is usually cited as the more comedic of the duo.
D) and Costello is usually cited as the more comedic of the duo.

Mono was no joke. Claira had now missed several weeks of school, and her mother was paranoid that she would fall behind. **19** Luckily, the teacher gave Claira her notes.

19

A) NO CHANGE
B) Luckily, the notes were given to Claira by her.
C) Luckily, the teacher's notes were available for Claira.
D) Luckily, her notes were given to Claira.

Noun Agreement Error

Noun agreement errors arise when the numbers of corresponding nouns don't match up correctly. The way to fix noun agreement errors is to make sure the nouns match in number:

Incorrect

Comparative Literature and Classical Philosophy are an example of college majors that are unlikely to prepare you for a real job.

Fast-food restaurants support the cause of financial independence for teenagers by providing many with respectable jobs as a deep-fat fryer operator.

Correct

Comparative Literature and Classical Philosophy are examples of college majors that are unlikely to prepare you for a real job.

Fast-food restaurants support the cause of financial independence for teenagers by providing many with respectable jobs as deep-fat fryer operators.

The junior partners at this law firm have evolved into capable, resourceful litigators **34** from an inexperienced and uncertain clerk just two years before.

34

A) NO CHANGE
B) from the inexperienced and uncertain clerks they were just two years ago
C) in just two years from an inexperienced and uncertain clerk
D) when in just two years they were inexperienced and uncertain clerks

Joining a grassroots movement against unfair business practices, some citizens in the United States have begun protesting laws in the financial industry that protect unscrupulous people as **35** essentially an unknowing participant.

35

A) NO CHANGE
B) in essence, an unknowing participant
C) essentially unknowing participants
D) essential unknowing participants

Throughout the school year the teacher would often remind us that the best students are not those who possess innate ability but those who strive as **36** a partaker in a collective effort.

36

A) NO CHANGE
B) one of many partakers
C) partakers
D) partaking

Context and Flow

The SAT knows that many students read as little as possible when they're working through the Writing and Language test. As a result, they construct answer choices that are entirely plausible if – and only if – you don't pay attention to adjacent text.

As a result, you're going to need to acknowledge this and expand your window when you're dealing with questions regarding context and flow.

How will you know you're dealing with these types of questions? Well, they'll fall into three rather predictable categories that are pretty easy to identify:

1. **Conjunctions and Transitions:** These types of questions test whether you're paying attention to the ideas contained in the passage and whether you know how to link ideas together in a logical way. You're going to have to read surrounding sentences here, especially if you're starting or finishing a paragraph.
2. **Combining Sentences:** If you're linking two sentences to each other, the combination must be grammatically sound (obviously), but must also acknowledge any shifts in thought AND be elegantly written. No big deal.
3. **Sentence or Paragraph Placement:** You may occasionally see [1], [2], [3], etc. labelling sentences or paragraphs within a passage. If so, you may be asked to move around a sentence or paragraph to another place that makes more sense.

Reading for context and flow is all about understanding how thoughts should be structured and ordered so that the author's writing makes as much sense as possible.

The key is reading enough to know what all the thoughts are so you know how they should be ordered or linked.

Conjunctions and Transitions

Conjunctions are used to join parts of a sentence. They can (among other things) be used to indicate a continuation of a thought, set up a contrast, or denote a causal relationship. The conjunction has to operate logically in the sentence.

Incorrect

*We generally think of hamburgers and apple pie as quintessentially American foods, **and** both have their origins in European cuisine.*

*Craig was satisfied with the outcome of the case, **since** it wasn't the exact result he had hoped for.*

Correct

*We generally think of hamburgers and apple pie as quintessentially American foods, **but** both have their origins in European cuisine.*

*Craig was satisfied with the outcome of the case, **even though** it wasn't the exact result he had hoped for.*

There are a few different types of conjunctions, though they get tested in generally the same way.

First, we have **Coordinating Conjunctions: FANBOYS**

For

And

Nor

But

Or

Yet

So

These are the most common, simplest conjunctions. These words serve to introduce changes or continuations of thought within or between clauses or sentences. You must *read for meaning* to identify errors involving these words.

We also have **Subordinating Conjunctions**.

after	even if	than
although	even though	that
as	if	though
as if	in case	till
as long as	in order that	unless
as much as	lest	until
as soon as	once	when
as though	only if	whenever
because	provided that	where
before	since	wherever
by the time	so that	while

Don't go crazy trying to memorize this list. Coordinating conjunctions are obvious and only one or two will show up on any single test.

It took Ethan more than 48 hours of frustrating and persistent effort **10** and he finally finished the difficult video game.

A) NO CHANGE
B) before his finally finishing the difficult video game
C) but finally the difficult video game was finished
D) to finally finish the difficult video game

12 Because of repeatedly asking in vain for a meeting to discuss improved working conditions, the factory workers began to picket as a protest against their employer's intransigence.

A) NO CHANGE
B) After repeatedly asking in vain for a meeting to discuss improved working conditions,
C) They have repeatedly asked in vain for a meeting to discuss improved working conditions, then
D) While they repeatedly ask in vain for a meeting to discuss improved working conditions,

While for some people reality television is pure idiocy, to be ignored only because it encourages vapidity, **14** but for others a daily source of endless entertainment.

A) NO CHANGE
B) but for others it is
C) and for others is
D) for others it is

Inter-Sentence & Inter-paragraph Transitions

In addition to maintaining consistency of thought *within* a sentence, conjunctions and transition words are often necessary to smooth conceptual connections *between* sentences and paragraphs.

Studies warned that catastrophic global outcomes are sure to result from an average temperature increase of as little as 2°C. **2** Consequently, current projections suggest that this future is all but guaranteed.

2

A) NO CHANGE
B) However
C) Unfortunately
D) Henceforth

Fine woodworking requires hand tools to be properly tuned to be most effective. **4** However, any serious craftsman will spend time calibrating and honing a chisel before using it for the first time.

4

A) NO CHANGE
B) For example,
C) In spite of this,
D) Nevertheless,

The candidate, though a heavy favorite, lost the election by the narrowest of margins.

7 National elections in this country have always been part policy discussion, part popularity contest; indeed, few analysts correctly predicted the outcome of the election.

7

Which choice best connects the sentence with the previous paragraph?

A) NO CHANGE
B) The candidate's loss struck many by surprise
C) Presidential elections are held every four years
D) To win a presidential election, a candidate must secure 270 electoral votes

Combining Sentences

Combining sentence is part art and part science.

> The sentences will have to be joined in a way that is *grammatically correct*. Watch out for **Sentence Fragments**, **Comma Splices**, and **Misplaced Modifiers**.
>
> You'll also have to ensure the *logical flow of thoughts*. That means you'll need to pay attention to **Conjunctions** and **Transition Words**.
>
> Lastly, the answer choice you select should be *elegantly worded*. That means you'll need to apply **KISS KIM.**

That's a lot, so let's practice.

In addition to this, the show is not

12 scripted. However the general plot of each scene is outlined, and the actors improvise the actual conversations.

12

Which choice most effectively combines the two sentences at the underlined portion?

A) scripted,

B) scripted, and then

C) scripted; and

D) scripted, but rather

Although, in the 1950's, huge waves of African Americans migrated to Newark from the rural

20 south. Due to structural causes and discrimination, there was a dearth of jobs awaiting them.

20

Which choice most effectively combines the two sentences at the underlined portion?

A) south, but due

B) south; due

C) south, due

D) south, and due

According to the accident log, the car was traveling twenty miles over the speed **27** limit. This was revealed by the car's onboard computer.

27

Which choice most effectively combines the two sentences at the underlined portion?

A) limit as

B) limit, and this speed can be

C) limit, which can also be

D) limit when the speed is

Sentence and Paragraph Placement

A surprising number of questions on the Writing & Language Test require you to use critical reading skills. If you're asked to move a sentence or paragraph, there are a few things you'll need to pay attention to:

- **Specialized Language:** If the passage uses language that wouldn't be accessible to the layman, chances are the term will be defined somewhere in the passage. The definition of the term should always be before it's used without explanation.

- **Transitional Phrases or Conjunctions:** Phrases such as "for instance", "as a result", or "to his surprise" indicate a connection between sentences. The sentence placement must make sense.

- **Chronological Triggers:** The SAT will never be so kind as to use "first", "second", and "last"; however, the test will occasionally use time indicators such as dates or "*x* weeks ago" to help you orient the sentences or paragraphs.

- **Pronouns:** Pronoun ambiguity occurs when the writer uses a pronoun without making clear what that pronoun refers to. If a sentence uses the word *it* or *this*, the prior sentence had better be about that thing (and nothing else).

[1] Urban planning is an interesting challenge. [2] This term refers to the fact that there are often multiple decision-makers who each have conflicting imperatives and desires. [3] While the design process of many infrastructure projects – such as bridges, highways, and power lines – is primarily constrained by geological features, zoning restrictions, and building material attributes, urban roadway design is often referred to as a "wicked problem." [4] Each of the design choices is often a zero-sum game: in order for one group to get what it wants, another must make a sacrifice. **4** **5**

4

To make this paragraph most logical, sentence 2 should be

A) placed where it is now.

B) placed before sentence 1.

C) placed before sentence 4.

D) DELETED from the paragraph.

5

To improve the cohesion and flow of this paragraph, the writer wants to add the following sentence.

> This characteristic often requires policymakers to prioritize one group's needs over another's.

The sentence would most logically be placed after

A) sentence 2.

B) sentence 3.

C) sentence 4.

D) sentence 5.

If a question is about paragraph placement, determine which answer choice most logically facilitates the logical flow of the passage. It's always a good idea to pay attention to topic sentences and look for transitional language.

[1]

Washington, D.C. is an illustrative example. It's a great place to visit, but I can't recommend living there. The layout of the streets makes sense on paper, with a strong emphasis placed on public transportation and walking, but navigating the city in a car can be a total nightmare. Constant construction and renovations result in gridlock and travel delays. Inadequate or contradictory road signage is particularly confusing for nonnative drivers. Cyclists and brazen pedestrians pose a constant threat. The road system was designed in 1791 by Pierre L'Enfant, a French-born architect and city planner. The infrastructure doesn't seem to be capable of handling the volume of drivers in the city.

[2]

Urban planning is an interesting challenge. While the design process of many infrastructure projects – such as bridges, highways, and power lines – is primarily constrained by geological features, zoning restrictions, and building material attributes, urban roadway design is often referred to as a "wicked problem." This term refers to the fact that there are often multiple decision-makers who each have conflicting imperatives and desires. Each of the design choices is often a zero-sum game: in order for one group to get what it wants, another must make a sacrifice.

[3]

You might think your worries are over once you're parked. You'd be wrong. While many drivers in the district can blow through red lights and exceed posted speed limits with relative impunity, heaven help you if you inadvertently disobey one of the unnecessarily complicated (and often contradictory) parking restrictions. One can't help but wonder whether funds intended for civil law enforcement are frequently diverted toward an already overstaffed parking enforcement battalion.

[4]

For instance, a pedestrian safety advocacy group may want additional crosswalk locations, lower speed limits, or narrower car lanes. These features, which will ostensibly improve a pedestrian's urban experience, will doubtless make things more difficult for delivery truck drivers and negatively impact the local businesses that rely on the deliveries those trucks are carrying. On the other hand, businesses that offer services rather than physical goods may actually prefer slower traffic flow because it might improve visibility to potential clients. Public officials must therefore carefully consider the potential outcomes of any decision before committing to a particular course of action.

What's the correct paragraph order? Why?

Answer: 2, 4, 1, 3

Reading Comprehension on Writing & Language

A handful of questions on the Writing & Language Test will seem like they got lost on their way to the Reading Test. These questions will require you to actually pay attention to the content of the passage.

They come in three general categories:

1. **Relevancy:** These are the most common. These types of questions will generally ask whether a certain phrase or sentence belongs in the passage. If the thought contained isn't directly related to the paragraph specifically or passage generally, it should be excised.
2. **Interpreting Graphs:** If the passage incorporates a graph or some other visual representation of data, the SAT will test your ability to interpret the information as it relates to the main idea of the passage. Read the chart carefully and you'll be just fine. You should expect to see one or two of these on any test.
3. **Main Idea:** You'll need to use the main idea to determine what type of sentence should be added to a passage. The questions themselves will usually give you some sort of directive as to what element of the passage you should prioritize. You'll see two or three of these per test.

Relevancy

Entertaining diversions have no place on the SAT. Every sentence that's in a passage should push the main idea forward and always be related to the main point of the paragraph.

Anecdotally, we have found that most of the time when you're asked whether it's appropriate to add a sentence to a passage, the answer is *no* because the additional information is irrelevant.

> **When in doubt, assume the additional information is unnecessary.**

If the additional information...	you should...
clarifies a term that is introduced in a previous sentence,	keep it.
describes a process that is referenced in a previous sentence,	keep it.
smooths a transition between two separate ideas,	keep it.
blurs the focus of the main idea of the passage,	delete it.
repeats an idea that is contained earlier in the passage,	delete it.
contradicts information that is contained earlier in the passage,	delete it.
introduces a fact that is chronologically out of order,	delete it.

Washington, D.C. is an illustrative example. It's a great place to visit, but I can't recommend living there. The layout of the streets makes sense on paper, with a strong emphasis placed on public transportation and walking, but navigating the city in a car can be a total nightmare. Constant construction and renovations result in gridlock and travel delays. Inadequate or contradictory road signage is particularly confusing for nonnative drivers. Cyclists and brazen pedestrians pose a constant threat. **7** The infrastructure doesn't seem to be capable of handling the volume of drivers in the city.

Times have changed drastically since Washington, DC's road design was conceptualized.

17

At this point, the writer is considering adding the following sentence.

> The road system was designed in 1791 by Pierre L'Enfant, a French-born architect and city planner.

Should the writer make this addition here?

A) Yes, because it helps clarify the paragraph's main message that the district's infrastructure is out of date.

B) Yes, because it clarifies a claim contained earlier in the paragraph regarding the road design.

C) No, because it blurs the focus of the paragraph by providing a detail that is out of place.

D) No, because the tone of the sentence is inconsistent with that of the rest of the passage.

Urban planning is an interesting challenge. While the design process of many infrastructure projects – such as bridges, highways, and power lines – is primarily constrained by geological features, zoning restrictions, and building material attributes, urban roadway design is often referred to as a "wicked problem." This term refers to the fact that there are often multiple decision-makers who each have conflicting imperatives and desires. Each of the design choices is often a zero-sum game: in order for one group to get what it wants, another must make a sacrifice. **3**

3

At this point, the writer is considering adding the following sentence.

> Other examples of zero-sum games include poker, arm-wrestling, and presidential elections.

Should the writer make this addition here?

A) Yes, because it helps clarify a technical term by providing additional illustrative examples.

B) Yes, because it reinforces the main point of the passage by providing a supporting example.

C) No, because it reiterates a definition that is provided earlier in the paragraph.

D) No, because it blurs the focus of the passages by providing examples that aren't clearly related to the topic of the passage.

Comedy, perhaps more than any other genre, relies on the identity of the audience to be effective. Ideas about what is funny vary immensely across cultures and generations. Effective comedy relies on knowledge of cultural norms, identities, expectations, traditions, values, and current and historical events, to name a few. The comedy "Curb Your Enthusiasm" skillfully manipulates these things, not only to simply create humorous situations, but also to reveal the humor of these expected and accepted aspects of society. In doing so, the show is not just a comedy; it is social commentary on the customs and habits of Americans and their everyday interactions. **33**

Because each show is only about thirty minutes long, the audience can expect with the start of every new scene to find out what exactly is funny about the scene and what it reveals about society.

33

The writer is considering deleting the underlined sentence. Should the sentence be kept or deleted?

A) Kept, because it provides a crucial logical connection to the point discussed in the following paragraph.

B) Kept, because it explains why the show is so effective as a comedy and why its viewers continue to watch.

C) Deleted, because it blurs the focus of the paragraph by introducing loosely related information.

D) Deleted, because it contradicts a claim made earlier in the paragraph.

Interpreting Graphs

You may have heard of the ACT. It's the SAT's biggest competitor. More and more students are taking the ACT because it has a reputation for being a fairer test. Whether it actually is a fairer test is another story...

Anyway, the biggest difference between the two tests is that the ACT has a science portion. Lots of charts and graphs and interpreting results. It's pretty great.

ETS wanted to get in on that hot visual representation of data action, but couldn't be bothered creating an actual new test section, so they tacked on a handful of half-assed graph interpretation questions as part of the Reading Test. Big whoop.

There's not much to these questions. Chart questions on the Math Test are significantly more difficult. Just be sure to read the chart title, axis labels, and any footnotes.

...as the chart shows, viewers in the 18-34 year age group have consistently **18** watched less and less NFL since 2011. These findings suggest that **19** declines in viewership for the NFL have been less pronounced for 18-34 year olds compared with the overall population since 2011.

% Change in NFL Viewership by Age Group, 2011-2016

■ % change in NFL viewership among 18-34 year olds
■ % change in NFL viewership for all age groups

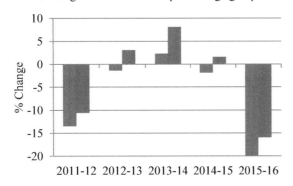

Year NFL Season

Adapted from "Switch Off the Football" by Leila Abboud, © 2016 Bloomberg News

18

Which choice offers an accurate interpretation of the data in the graph?

A) NO CHANGE
B) watched the NFL at nearly the same levels as viewer from all age groups.
C) watched the NFL in consistently lower levels than viewers in all age groups since 2011.
D) had smaller increases and bigger decreases in NFL viewership than viewers in all age groups since 2011.

19

Which choice offers an accurate interpretation of the data in the graph?

A) NO CHANGE
B) declines in viewership for the NFL have been more pronounced for 18-34 year olds compared with the overall population since 2011.
C) declines in viewership for the NFL have been more pronounced for the overall population compared with 18-34 year olds since 2011.
D) declines in viewership for the NFL have been equally pronounced for both 18-34 years and the overall viewing population since 2011.

Main Idea

We're going to go ahead and treat these types of questions as Critical Reading questions, which means – you guessed it – answering the questions in our own words whenever possible.

Pay attention to the passage. Occasionally ask yourself,

"Why would someone feel compelled to write this?"

Urban Road Planning: a "Wicked Problem"

Urban planning is an interesting challenge. While the design process of many infrastructure projects – such as bridges, highways, and power lines – is primarily constrained by geological features, zoning restrictions, and building material attributes, urban roadway design is often referred to as a "wicked problem." This term refers to the fact that there are often multiple decision-makers who each have conflicting imperatives and desires. Each of the design choices is often a zero-sum game: in order for one group to get what it wants, another must make a sacrifice.

For instance, a pedestrian safety advocacy group may want additional crosswalk locations, lower speed limits, or narrower car lanes. These features, which will ostensibly improve a pedestrian's urban experience, will doubtless make things more difficult for delivery truck drivers and negatively impact the local businesses that rely on the deliveries those trucks are carrying. On the other hand, businesses that offer services rather than physical goods may actually prefer slower traffic flow because it might improve visibility to potential clients. **4** Public officials must therefore carefully consider the potential outcomes of any decision before committing to a particular course of action.

4

Which choice most clearly ends the paragraph with a restatement of the writer's primary claim?

A) NO CHANGE
B) Business owners will often look for ways to subtly influence policymakers so that the local government will enact policies that are beneficial to businesses.
C) Surprisingly, cities with more efficient public transportation systems often experience similar levels of congestion and traffic.
D) Experts agree that until autonomous vehicles are put into mass production, traffic issues will likely continue to plague most major cities.

Washington, D.C. is an illustrative example. It's a great place to visit, but I can't recommend living there. The layout of the streets makes sense on paper, with a strong emphasis placed on public transportation and walking, but navigating the city in a car can be a total nightmare. Constant construction and renovations result in gridlock and travel delays. Inadequate or contradictory road signage is particularly confusing for nonnative drivers. Cyclists and brazen pedestrians pose a constant threat. The road system was designed in 1791 by Pierre L'Enfant, a French-born architect and city planner. The infrastructure doesn't seem to be capable of handling the volume of drivers in the city.

You might think your worries are over once you're parked. You'd be wrong. While many drivers in the district can blow through red lights and exceed posted speed limits with relative impunity, heaven help you if you inadvertently disobey one of the unnecessarily complicated (and often contradictory) parking restrictions. One can't help but wonder whether funds intended for civil law enforcement are frequently diverted toward an already overstaffed parking enforcement battalion. **11** Perhaps in the future the urban planners will pay more attention to the needs of drivers in the district and less to wringing as many fines as possible out of people who have no choice but to drive there.

11

The writer wants a conclusion that conveys how the tradeoffs discussed earlier in the passage have played a role in Washington, DC. Which choice best accomplishes this goal?

A) NO CHANGE
B) In the case of Washington, DC, it appears that policymakers who valued the concerns of drivers lost out to those for whom raising revenue was paramount.
C) Driving in Washington, DC may never be as convenient as taking advantage of the district's public transportation options, but many drivers simply don't have that option.
D) Given the choice between driving in Washington, DC and using public transportation, many commuters would no doubt choose the latter.

Good Writing vs. Bad Writing

Approximately 15% of the questions on the Writing and Language Test will look like grammar questions but present four answer choices that are grammatically correct.

What gives?

Well, on these types of questions, the SAT is testing your ability to identify good writing. Since the word "good" is subjective, we'll need to define it a bit more objectively.

On the SAT, good writing has the following qualities:

1. **Maintains Appropriate Word Choice:** The vocabulary and syntax matches the tone of the passage and the words have the correct dictionary definition.
2. **Avoids Wordiness & Preserves the Author's Intended Meaning:** Generally, the fewer words you need to use, the better. Also, don't change the author's message. That's messed up.
3. **Avoids Redundancy:** Redundancy occurs when you use different words to repeat yourself and say the same thing twice. Annoying, right?

The following modules will explore each of these characteristics in more detail.

Word Choice

Ah. *Le mot juste*. On the SAT, you'll occasionally be presented with a list of substitutes that all mean *roughly* the same thing. In these cases, you're being tested on your knowledge of two attributes of a word:

> **Denotation:** the dictionary definition of the word
>
> **Connotation:** the feelings or emotions that a word elicits

Being good and denotation questions means being comfortable with the dictionary. For instance, which of these two is correct?

A) My boss inferred that he was unhappy with my work when he told me he wasn't looking forward to my evaluation.

B) My boss implied that he was unhappy with my work when he told me he wasn't looking forward to my evaluation.

That's denotation. Connotation is a bit more subtle. Consider the words "mother" and "mommy." Both refer to the same thing, but the word choice tells you a lot about the speaker.

Give that kid an apple.
And maybe a hug.

Run.

On the SAT, identifying the correct answer on **denotation** questions means knowing what words mean. Just because words are synonyms, related, or look alike doesn't mean you can use them interchangeably. And you thought the SAT wasn't testing vocabulary anymore…

When asked to participate in the evening's festivities, she quickly gave her **13** ascent and accepted the invitation.

13

A) NO CHANGE
B) assent
C) advent
D) assertion

Consequently, the judge had no choice but to take decisive action and **17** condemn the defendant's actions.

17

A) NO CHANGE
B) condone
C) convict
D) commend

The flamenco guitar style is characterized by a thinner top and less internal bracing. These features help to **21** procure a brighter and more percussive sound than other types of classical guitar.

21

A) NO CHANGE
B) induce
C) secure
D) produce

Connotation questions are all about matching the tone of the passage. Since it's the SAT and every passage feels like it was written by a robot, that usually just means avoiding slang or colloquial expressions.

The researchers determined that securing funding for their next big project would only be

16 a piece of cake if they could demonstrate the financial viability of the new treatment.

A) NO CHANGE
B) feasible
C) doable
D) a snap

The voters decided to reelect the incumbent politician when she **22** vowed to push forward the progressive agenda she used to win the election.

22

A) NO CHANGE
B) subscribed
C) insisted
D) asserted

KISS KIM

Fun fact: when *Hamlet*'s Polonius said "Brevity is the soul of wit", he was actually talking about the SAT. Surprised you didn't know that.

Good Writing	Bad Writing
active voice	passive voice
preserves the author's intended meaning	changes the author's intended meaning
succinct	wordy
verbs for verbs	nouns instead of verbs

Remember this handy mnemonic:

Keep

It

Short and

Sweet

Keep the

Intended

Meaning[1]

---

[1] Not Kardashian. She nasty.[2]

[2] This book will have to be amended very soon because you won't know who she is.

In the article, it focused on the potential health benefits of regular tea consumption. **13**

13

A) NO CHANGE
B) In the article, its focus was the potential health benefits of regular tea consumption.
C) The article focused on the potential health benefits of regular tea consumption.
D) The focus of the article was on the potential health benefits of regular tea consumption, and what they might be.

Francis Scott Key composed the American national anthem "The Star-Spangled Banner" in 1814 with his purpose being to recount **16** the bombardment of Fort McHenry by the British Royal Navy.

16

A) NO CHANGE
B) and his purpose was recounting
C) to recount
D) he recounted

 When in doubt, go with the shorter Answer Choice.

Redundancy

In real life, it's OK to occasionally repeat yourself. Pobody's nerfect.

On the SAT, however, expressing the same idea twice within a sentence is a big no-no. Redundancy errors are fairly rare – you should only expect to see one or two per test.

Incorrect

Scientists expect Halley 's Comet to reappear again in 2061, as the comet passes within unaided view of Earth approximately every 75 years or so.

Correct

Scientists expect Halley 's Comet to reappear in 2061, as the comet passes within unaided view of Earth approximately every 75 years.

By switching to low power compact fluorescent bulbs, the company was able to realize annual savings on its utility expenses of nearly two thousand dollars **24** per year.

24
A) NO CHANGE
B) every year.
C) each year.
D) DELETE the underlined portion and end the sentence with a period.

Most of the actor's most **26** famous roles revolved around spouting obnoxious catch phrases and nearly negating earlier years of respectable thespianism.

26
A) NO CHANGE
B) famous and well-known
C) famous and commonly known
D) famous, commonly known

Many of the world's most famous entrepreneurs **28** initially began their careers as low-level employees at larger companies, which allowed them to learn the ropes of the industry while assuming less risk.

28
A) NO CHANGE
B) start to begin their careers
C) initiate their development
D) began their careers

Study Sheet

Yeah, we're tired of typing. You fill this out.

General Strategy

Goal Scores:

How questions can you guess on?

What are the three key determinants of your score?

When should you use the Answer Choices to help?

When shouldn't you use the Answer Choices to help?

What is the **Two Pass System**?

Math

Strategy

How do you use Order of Difficulty to improve your performance?

Why is your pencil your best friend on the SAT?

How should you set up your workspace on every question?

Algebra

What are some phrases in Word Problems that you'll have to watch out for?

What are the five strategies for *Working with Multiple Unknowns*?

Geometry

What are the steps of the Geometry Approach?

Functions and Graphs

What are the three general types of Function Questions?

What are the three forms of *Quadratic Functions*?

Reading

What are the steps to the Reading Approach?

What symbols do you use to mark the Answer Choices on Reading? What do they mean?

What are the two broad types of Reading Questions?

What are the three types of Reading Passages?

Writing & Language

What are the four categories of questions on the Writing & Language test? Describe each.

List the Grammar Rules tested on the Writing & Language Test.

The Week of the Test

The test will fall on a Saturday (or a Sunday if you have certain special accommodations). Here is what you should be doing the week leading up to the test.

Monday

Reread the General Strategy Modules and review the technique for the Reading test.

Tuesday

Review the Algebra, Arithmetic, and Geometry modules in this book. Focus on the areas that you have had the most trouble with.

Wednesday

Review the four question types for the Writing & Language test. Review the Grammar Rules. Get to bed an hour early.

Thursday

Review the Functions & Graphs and Statistics modules in this book. Get to bed an hour early.

Friday

No studying! Relax. Set out the materials you'll need for the test:

1. SAT registration ticket
2. Photo ID
3. Calculator (with fresh batteries)
4. Three #2 pencils (mechanical pencils are NOT allowed on the test)
5. Snack (granola bar or something similar is best)
6. Beverage in a re-sealable container
7. Pack of gum
8. Directions to the test center (if necessary)

Watch a fun movie or read a book – nothing too heavy. Relax.

Get to bed an hour early. Set your alarm for no later than 6:30. You'll need to be at the test center by 7:45am at the latest.

The Morning of the Test

Eat breakfast. You'll be stuck in the testing center until 1pm and don't want your mind focused on your stomach. While you're eating, take out your Official SAT Study Guide and work through a few questions to warm up before you get to the test center.

Dress comfortably and wear layers. You don't know what the testing room will be like.

When you get to the testing center, power down your mobile phone or leave it in the car.

When you enter the testing room, follow the proctor's instructions, particularly when he or she is guiding you through filling out the student information.

Before the test begins, take a deep breath, relax, and remind yourself that you know a lot about the SAT – probably more about the test than anyone else in the room. Take comfort in that fact.

If you have any issues during the test (e.g., noises outside of the classroom, proctor doesn't keep time correctly, uncomfortable testing environment, etc.), respectfully ask the proctor if there's any way the problem can be addressed. It's the proctor's job to make your testing experience smooth and as pleasant as possible.

During the Test

Use the concepts and techniques you learned in this book. Don't fall back into your old habits. Everything you learned has been tested and really works on the SAT. If you encounter a section that totally kicks your butt, chances are that it is the experimental section and won't count towards your score. Keep calm and test on.

After the Test

Relax. It's over. Scores will be available online the third Thursday after the test.

When you get your scores back, let us know how you did! Shoot us an email at contact@specifixprep.com and tell us your story. We value your feedback and experiences to help make our product as helpful as possible.

Assignment	Date Due	Status

Assignment	Date Due	Status

Made in the USA
Middletown, DE
17 October 2018